PERFECT PHRASES

in Spanish

for

GARDENING

and LANDSCAPING

**500+ Essential Words and Phrases
for Communicating with Spanish-Speakers**

Jean Yates

New York Chicago San Francisco Lisbon London Madrid Mexico City
Milan New Delhi San Juan Seoul Singapore Sydney Toronto

Library of Congress Cataloging-in-Publication Data

Yates, Jean.
      Perfect phrases in Spanish for gardening and landscaping / Jean Yates.
         p.   cm. — (Perfect phrases)
      ISBN 0-07-149477-4 (alk. paper)
      1. Spanish language—Conversation and phrase books (for
gardeners).   2. Spanish language—Conversation and phrase books (for
landscaping industry employees).   3. Gardening—Terminology.   I. Title.

      PC4120.G35Y38   2007
      468.3′421024635—dc22   2007039858

1 2 3 4 5 6 7 8 9 10 11 12 13 14 15 16 17 18 19 20 21   DOC/DOC 0 9 8

ISBN 978-0-07-149477-9
MHID   0-07-149477-4

McGraw-Hill books are available at special quantity discounts to use as premiums and sales promotions or for use in corporate training programs. To contact a representative, please visit the Contact Us pages at www.mhprofessional.com.

This book is printed on acid-free paper.

Contents

Contents

CHAPTER 2: ESTABLISHING POLICIES   33

CHAPTER 3: GENERAL INSTRUCTIONS FOR LANDSCAPING WORK   47

Contents

Contents

Introduction

In many parts of the United States, individuals and companies are employing at an increasing rate Spanish-speaking landscape workers, gardeners, and lawn-care crews who do not speak English. This book is designed to provide employers with simple phrases in Spanish that will enable them to communicate basic information to their employees, helping to ensure that they understand the information necessary for jobs to be done correctly, efficiently, and safely. In learning some Spanish phrases, employers often develop stronger working relationships with their employees, who are generally most appreciative of this interest.

It is very common for people who do not speak each others' languages to communicate with hand signals, gestures, or words they may have heard others say. This may lead to a certain level of mutual understanding, but it is certainly less than ideal, especially in a job setting, as it often ends in misunderstandings by both parties, can cause mishaps and bad feelings, and could even be dangerous. In this book, employers will find key words and phrases that will help them begin communicating with their Spanish-speaking employees in a clear and correct manner right from the beginning. While this is not a course in grammar or conversation, those who consistently use these words and phrases with their employees will find that they are beginning to understand and use quite a bit of Spanish, and can actually build on this foundation to continue learning the language.

How This Book Is Organized

The phrases in this book are divided into six sections. In Chapter 1, you will find general words and expressions that are used every day to say such things as hello and good-bye, please and thank you, and other common courtesies. Also in this section are the phrases that will enable you to both hire and terminate help and to explain to an employee the general rules and policies of employment with you, including such topics as wages, Social Security payments, punctuality, and so forth. You will also find the words to help you express satisfaction or dissatisfaction with an employee's performance. In Chapter 2, you will find phrases for introducing your business to a potential employee and establishing the basic policies that you set regarding working for you. Chapter 3 includes expressions for giving general instructions that tell the way you would like things to be done. Chapter 4 provides specific expressions for carrying out the tasks normally required for new landscaping projects. Chapter 5 provides phrases related to the maintenance of outdoor areas. The Appendix consists of a table of the numbers from 0 to 1,000,000, for handy reference, followed by two glossaries of all the words used in the book arranged in alphabetical order, the first from English to Spanish, and the second from Spanish to English.

Vocabulary Guidelines

Throughout the book there are phrases that allow for substitutable words. When this occurs, the word that can be replaced with another is <u>underlined</u>. Then one, two, or more words that could easily replace the underlined word are presented. This feature will help you memorize the most useful phrases, and generate an unlimited number of useful sentences. An example is shown in the following:

Please plant <u>the trees</u>.	**Por favor, plantee <u>los árboles</u>.**
	(por fah-BOR, plahn-TEH-eh lohs AHR-boh-less)
the bushes	**los arbustos**
	(lohs ar-BOO-stohs)
the flowers	**las flores**
	(lahs FLOR-ess)

Pronunciation Guidelines

Each phrase in Chapter 1 and Chapter 2 is printed in Spanish to the right of its equivalent English phrase, with a guide to its pronunciation written directly underneath. The symbols used are an approximation of how the words would sound if they were written in English, as illustrated below.

Vowels

To make a Spanish vowel sound, open your mouth and place your lips in position, and do not move your lips until you make the next sound.

Spanish Spelling	Approximate Pronunciation
a	ah
e	eh
i	ee
o	oh
u	oo

To make a vowel combination, begin with the first vowel, then move your lips into the position of the second.

ai	eye
ei	ay (like the *ei* in *weight*)
oi	oy
ui	wee
ia	yah
ie	yeh
io	yoh
iu	yoo
au	ahoo
eu	ehoo
ua	wah
ue	weh
uo	woh

Consonants

b	b
ca / co / cu	kah / koh / koo
ce / ci	seh / see
d (to begin a word)	d
d (after a vowel)	th (as in *brother*)
f	f
ga / go / gu	gah / goh / goo
ge / gi	heh / hee
h	silent (like the *h* in *honest*)
j	h

la / le / li / lo / lu	lah / leh / lee / loh / loo
al / el / il / ol / ul	adl / edl / eedl / odl / udl
ll	y / j
m	m
n	n
n (before c / g)	ng (like the *ng* in *finger*)
ña / ñe / ñi / ño / ñu	n'yah / n'yeh / n'yee / n'yoh / n'yoo
p	p
que / qui	keh / kee
r (at the beginning)	rrr (trilled)
r (between vowels)	d / tt / dd
bari	body
beri	Betty
biri	beady
ora	oughtta
vuru	voodoo
rr	rrr (trilled)
s	s
t	t
v	b
x	ks
y	y / j
z	s

Syllables

As a general rule, each syllable that is printed in lowercase letters should be pronounced with the same tone and length, and the syllable printed in capital letters should be emphasized, by saying it a little louder and longer than the others. For example, the word, *bueno*, which means "good," is represented as follows:

good   **bueno**
          (B'WEH-noh)

How to Get the Most out of This Book

There are many ways that you can help build your Spanish vocabulary:

- Use the pronunciation guidelines provided, but also listen to your employees and try to copy their pronunciation.
- Customize your phrases by substituting words with other words from the lists provided, and also with new words you may learn from your employees. Words that are underlined can be substituted with words from the alphabetical lists provided in the glossaries.
- Keep a notebook—ask your employees to say or write down problematical words or expressions; then, if you cannot find the words in this book, seek help from a dictionary or a bilingual speaker.
- To learn new words from your employees, begin right away by memorizing the following question:

How do you say _____   **¿Cómo se dice _____ en español?**
 in Spanish?   (KOH-moh seh DEE-seh _____ en
            eh-spahn-YOHL)

The words you get as answers to your question can be added to your notebook to help you remember them.

Cultural Guidelines

In most Spanish-speaking countries, there are three ways to say *you*: **tú**, to a person you generally socialize with; **usted**, to any other person, including a person you work for or who works for you, and **ustedes**, to two or more people whom you are talking to at the same time. The phrases in this book are given in the **usted** form, and instructions are also provided for changing these to the plural **ustedes** form. This will ensure that you are speaking to your employees in a respectful manner that will certainly be appreciated. Employees will also respond to you with this form.

Some Hispanic cultures have a more relaxed concept of time than that generally accepted in the United States. You will need to make it clear that arriving on time and on the agreed day(s), especially for work, is very important here, and that if an emergency arises that causes an employee to be late or unable to work, you expect to be informed right away.

You may want to have some idea about the family situations of your employees, as family is generally very important in Hispanic culture. Your workers may be supporting a number of family members both here and back home. Be sure to make clear to those who work for you what your policies are for time off for family emergencies and celebrations as well as for personal illness. You may also wish to state right from the beginning your feelings about family members accompanying or visiting your employee while on the job.

Chapter 1

Spanish Basics

E xchanging pleasantries and greetings with your Spanish-speaking employees is a great way to begin to build a stronger working relationship.

Greetings

The following are the most common ways to greet people and to say good-bye to them.

Hello.	**Hola.**
	(OH-lah)
Good morning.	**Buenos días.**
	(B'WEH-nohs DEE-ahs)
Good afternoon.	**Buenas tardes.**
	(B'WEH-nahs TAR-thess)
Good evening.	**Buenas noches.**
	(B'WEH-nahs NOH-chess)
Good night.	**Buenas noches.**
	(B'WEH-nahs NOH-chess)
Good-bye.	**Adiós.**
	(ah—TH'YOHS)

See you later.	**Hasta luego.**
	(AH-stahl WEH-goh)
Have a nice day.	**Que le vaya bien.** (*lit*: May all go well
	for you—to someone who is
	leaving)
	(keh leh BAH-yah B'YEN)

In Spanish sometimes you need to change your greeting, depending on whether you are speaking to a male or a female and also when you speak to several people together. In the examples below, you'll see four ways to say "Welcome":

Welcome. (to a male)	**Bienvenido.**
	(b'yen beh-NEE-thoh)
Welcome. (to a female)	**Bienvenida.**
	(b'yen beh-NEE-thah)
Welcome. (to an all-male or	**Bienvenidos.**
mixed group)	(b'yen beh-NEE-thohs)
Welcome. (to an all-female group)	**Bienvenidas.**
	(b'yen beh-NEE-thahs)

Pleasantries

Just as "Hi, how are you?" is usually the first thing we say to each other in English, its equivalent in Spanish is the most usual greeting.

How are you?	**¿Cómo está?**
	(KOHM-weh-STAH?)

To say the same thing to more than one person, just add **n** to **está**, making **están**:

| How are you (all)? | **¿Cómo están?** |
| | (KOHM weh-STAHN?) |

Here are some stock answers:

Fine, thank you.	**Bien, gracias.**
	(B'YEN, GRAHS-yahs)
So-so.	**Regular.**
	(reh-goo-LAHR)
	Más o menos. (*lit*: more or less)
	(MAHS oh MEH-nos)
Not well.	**Mal.**
	(MAHL)

Family and Friends

"Family first" is an important concept in Hispanic culture, and asking about the health of family members is one way of showing that you understand and appreciate this.

Use the following formula to ask about one person:

| How is your <u>mother</u>? | **¿Cómo está su <u>mamá</u>?** |
| | (KOHM-weh-STAH soo mah-MAH) |

Just substitute any of the following words to ask about others:

father	**papá**
	(pah-PAH)
husband	**esposo**
	(eh-SPOH-soh)

3

wife	**esposa**
	(eh-SPOH-sah)
sister	**hermana**
	(her-MAH-nah)
brother	**hermano**
	(her-MAH-noh)
son	**hijo**
	(EE-hoh)
daughter	**hija**
	(EE-hah)

To inquire about more than one person at a time, just add **s** to **su**, another **s** to make the word plural, and add **n** to **está**:

How are your <u>parents</u>?	**¿Cómo están sus <u>papás</u>?**
	(KOHM-weh-STAHN soos pah-PAHS)
children	**hijos**
	(EE-hohs)
daughters	**hijas**
	(EE-hahs)
sisters and brothers	**hermanos**
	(ehr-MAH-nohs)
sisters	**hermanas**
	(ehr-MAH-nahs)

While we're on the subject of people important to us, let's include a few more who we can't do without:

friend (male)	**amigo**
	(ah-MEE-goh)

friend (female)	**amiga**
	(ah-MEE-gah)
boyfriend	**novio**
	(NOH-b'yoh)
girlfriend	**novia**
	(NOH-b'yah)
boss (male)	**patrón** / **jefe**
	(pah-TROHN) / (HEH-feh)
boss (female)	**patrona** / **jefa**
	(pah-TROH-nah) / (HEH-fah)
neighbor (male)	**vecino**
	(beh-SEE-noh)
neighbor (female)	**vecina**
	(beh-SEE-nah)

These words can also be made plural, by adding **s** (or **es** in the case of **patrón**). (It's probably not a good idea to make **novio** or **novia** plural.)

The "Magic" Words

These are the essential words for showing courtesy and respect. Memorize these right away.

Please.	**Por favor.**
	(por fah-BOR)
Thank you.	**Gracias.**
	(GRAH-s'yahs)
You're welcome.	**De nada.**
	(deh NAH-thah)

Excuse me.	**Disculpe.**
	(dees-KOOL-peh)
I'm sorry.	**Lo siento.**
	(loh S'YEN-toh)

Telling Present Time and Using Numbers 1–12

In the following section, you will find phrases for asking and telling the time. The numbers from 1–12, which you will need for other purposes as well, are introduced here.

What time is it?	**¿Qué hora es?**
	(KEH OH-rah ess)

This question is answered for *one o'clock* by the phrase:

It's one o'clock.	**Es la una.**
	(ess lah OO-nah)

For all other hours, use the following phrase, inserting a number between two and twelve:

It's <u>two</u> o'clock.	**Son las <u>dos</u>.**
	(sohn lahs DOHS)
three	**tres**
	(TRESS)
four	**cuatro**
	(K'WAH-troh)
five	**cinco**
	(SEENG-koh)

6

six	**seis**
	(SACE) (rhymes with *face*)
seven	**siete**
	(S'YEH-teh)
eight	**ocho**
	(OH-choh)
nine	**nueve**
	(N'WEH-beh)
ten	**diez**
	(D'YESS)
eleven	**once**
	(OHN-seh)
twelve	**doce**
	(DOH-seh)

For times in between the hours, use the following expressions:

It's one-fifteen.	**Es la una y cuarto.**
	(ess lah OO-nah ee K'WAHR-toh)
It's two-thirty.	**Son las dos y media.**
	(sohn lahs DOHS ee MEH-th'yah)
It's three-forty-five.	**Son las tres y cuarenta y cinco.**
	(sohn lahs TRESS ee k'wa-REN-ta ee SEENG-koh)

You can express *noon* and *midnight* as follows:

It's twelve o'clock noon.	**Es mediodía.**
	(ess meh-th'yoh DEE-ah)
It's midnight.	**Es medianoche.**
	(ess meh-th'yah NOH-cheh)

To indicate *morning*, add **de la mañana** to any hour:

It's ten A.M.

Son las diez de la mañana.
(sohn lahs D'YESS deh lah
mah-N'YAH-nah)

For afternoon or evening, add **de la tarde**:

It's four P.M.

Son las cuatro de la tarde.
(sohn lahs K'WAH-troh deh lah
TAHR-deh)

For night, add **de la noche**:

It's nine P.M.

Son las nueve de la noche.
(sohn lahs N'WEH-beh deh lah
NOH-cheh)

Indicating Work Hours

When you want someone to be somewhere or to do something at a particular time, use the following time expressions. Note that *one o'clock* is again slightly different from all the others:

at one o'clock

a la una
(ah lah OO-nah)

at two o'clock

a las dos
(ah lahs DOHS)

at four-thirty

a las cuatro y media
(ah lahs K'WAH-troh ee MEH-th'yah)

The concept of time may be a little fuzzier in Hispanic culture. The following expressions will indicate that you mean "gringo" time, that is, "on the dot." (And don't forget the "magic" **por favor**!)

Come tomorrow.	**Venga mañana.**
	(BENG-gah mah-N'YAH-nah)
Be here <u>at seven</u>.	**Esté aquí a las siete.**
	(es-STEH ah-KEE ah lahs S'YEH-teh)
on the dot	**en punto**
	(en POON-toh)
Be on time.	**Sea puntual.**
	(SEH-ah poon-TWAHL)
Come early.	**Venga temprano.**
	(BENG-gah tem-PRAH-noh)
Don't be late.	**No venga tarde.**
	(NOH BENG-gah TAHR-deh)
You will be finished at five o'clock.	**Terminará a las cinco.**
	(tehr-mee-nah-RAH ah lahs SEENG-koh)

Talking to More than One Person at a Time

Just as before, to give instructions to a group of people, just add **n** to the main word:

Come. (to one person)	**Venga.**
	(BENG-gah)
Come. (to two or more people)	**Vengan.**
	(BENG-gahn)

Be here. (to one person)	**Esté aquí.**
	(eh-STEH ah-KEE)
Be here. (to two or more people)	**Estén aquí.**
	(eh-STEN ah-KEE)

Days of the Week

If you look at a Spanish calendar, you will see that the extreme left-hand column is for Monday, rather than Sunday, as in the North American version. Sunday is put in the extreme right-hand column, putting the weekend days together. Most workers expect a free day a week, not necessarily on a weekend. This day is often referred to by workers as **mi día** (*my day*).

What day is today?	**¿Qué día es hoy?**
	(KEH DEE-ah ess OY)
Today is <u>Monday</u>.	**Hoy es <u>lunes</u>.**
	(OY ess LOO-ness)
Tomorrow is <u>Tuesday</u>.	**Mañana es <u>martes</u>.**
	(mah-N'YAH-nah es MAHR-tess)
Wednesday	**miércoles**
	(M'YEHR-koh-less)
Thursday	**jueves**
	(H'WEH-bess)
Friday	**viernes**
	(B'YER-ness)
Saturday	**sábado**
	(SAH-bah-thoh)
Sunday	**domingo**
	(doh-MEENG-goh)

To indicate a day in the future, add "el" before the name of the day:

Be here on Monday.

Esté aquí el lunes.

(eh-STEH ah-KEE el LOO-ness)

To indicate *always on that day*, add **los** before the name of the day:

Come on Mondays.

Venga los lunes.

(BENG-gah lohs LOO-ness)

Come every day.

Venga todos los días.

(BENG-gah TOH-thohs lohs DEE-ahs)

Don't come on Sundays.

No venga los domingos.

(NOH BENG-gah lohs

doh-MEENG-gohs)

Months of the Year and Using Numbers 1–31

Did you notice that the days of the week are not capitalized in Spanish? It's the same with the months. Also, when giving the date in abbreviated form, it is exactly the opposite from English. In other words, 3/9/08 in English would be March 9, 2008. In Spanish it would be the 3rd of September, 2008. Let's look at how these dates are written and said.

What's the date?

¿Cuál es la fecha?

(K'WAHL ess lah FEH-chah)

It's the first of January.

Es el primero de enero.

(ess el pree-MEH-roh deh

eh-NEH-roh)

After "the first" day, dates are given in cardinal numbers, as in "the 'two' of January," "the 'three' of January," and so forth. Following are examples using all of the months, and numbers up to thirty-one.

It's the <u>second</u> of <u>January</u>.	**Es el dos de enero.**
	(ess el DOHS deh-NEH-roh)
the third of February	**el tres de febrero**
	(el TRESS deh feh-BREH-roh)
the fourth of March	**el cuatro de marzo**
	(el K'WAH-troh deh MAHR-soh)
the fifth of April	**el cinco de abril**
	(el SEENG-koh deh ah-BREEL)
the sixth of May	**el seis de mayo**
	(el SACE deh MAH-yoh)
the seventh of June	**el siete de junio**
	(el S'YEH-teh deh HOON-yoh)
the eighth of July	**el ocho de julio**
	(el OH-choh de HOOL-yoh)
the ninth of August	**el nueve de agosto**
	(el N'WEH-beh deh ah-GOH-stoh)
the tenth of September	**el diez de septiembre**
	(el D'YESS deh sep-T'YEM-breh)
the eleventh of October	**el once de octubre**
	(el OHN-seh deh ohk-TOO-breh)
the twelfth of November	**el doce de noviembre**
	(el DOH-seh deh noh-B'YEM-breh)

the thirteenth of December	**el trece de diciembre**
	(el TREH-seh deh
	dee-S'YEM-breh)
the fourteenth	**el catorce**
	(el kah-TOR-seh)
the fifteenth	**el quince**
	(el KEEN-seh)
the sixteenth	**el dieciséis**
	(el d'yes-ee-SACE)
the seventeenth	**el diecisiete**
	(el d'yes-ee-S'YEH-teh)
the eighteenth	**el dieciocho**
	(el d'yes-YOH-choh)
the nineteenth	**el diecinueve**
	(el d'yes-ee-N'WEH-beh)
the twentieth	**el veinte**
	(el BAYN-teh)
the twenty-first	**el veintiuno**
	(el bayn-T'YOO-noh)
the twenty-second	**el veintidós**
	(el bayn-tee-DOHS)
the twenty-third	**el veintitrés**
	(el bayn-tee-TRESS)
the twenty-fourth	**el veinticuatro**
	(el bayn-tee-K'WAH-troh)
the twenty-fifth	**el veinticinco**
	(el bayn-tee-SEENG-koh)
the twenty-sixth	**el veintiséis**
	(el bayn-tee-SACE)

the twenty-seventh	**el veintisiete**
	(el bayn-tee-S'YEH-teh)
the twenty-eighth	**el veintiocho**
	(el bayn-T'YOH-choh)
the twenty-ninth	**el veintinueve**
	(el bayn-tee-N'WEH-beh)
the thirtieth	**el treinta**
	(el TRAYN-tah)
the thirty-first	**el treinta y uno**
	(el TRAYN-tah ee OO-noh)

Talking About the Weather

In outdoor work talking about the weather is more than just a pleasantry—it will most likely affect the work of the day. Following are the most common expressions.

How's the weather?	**¿Qué tiempo hace?**
	(KEH T'YEM-poh AH-seh)
It's fine.	**Hace buen tiempo.**
	(AH-seh B'WEHN T'YEM-poh)
It's hot.	**Hace calor.**
	(AH-seh kah-LOR)
It's cold.	**Hace frío.**
	(AH-seh FREE-oh)
It's raining.	**Está lloviendo.**
	(eh-STAH yoh-B'YEN-doh)
It's snowing.	**Está nevando.**
	(eh-STAH neh-BAHN-doh)
It's windy.	**Hace viento.**
	(AH-seh B'YEN-toh)

It's sunny.

Hace sol.

(AH-seh SOHL)

It's cloudy.

Está nublado.

(eh-STAH noo-BLAH-thoh)

There's a storm.

Hay una tormenta.

(EYE oo-nah tor-MEN-tah)

Interviewing an Employee

These are the phrases for learning the most basic information about your prospective employees.

What's your name?

¿Cuál es su nombre?

(K'WAHL ess soo NOHM-breh)

Where are you from?

¿De dónde es?

(deh THOHN-deh ess)

Where do you live?

¿Dónde vive?

(DOHN-deh BEE-beh)

How long have you been here?

¿Hace cuánto que vive aquí?

(AH-seh K'WAHN-toh keh BEE-beh
ah-KEE)

Where did you work before?

¿Dónde trabajó antes?

(DOHN-deh trah-bah-HOH AHN-tess)

What kind of work did you do?

¿Qué tipo de trabajo hizo?

(KEH TEE-poh deh trah-BAH-hoh
EE-soh)

Do you have any experience
  in outdoor work?

¿Ha trabajado afuera alguna vez?

(ha trah-bah-HAH-thoh ah-F'WEH-rah
ahl-goo-nah BESS)

Have you worked as a gardener before?	**¿Ha trabajado como jardinero alguna vez?**
	(ah trah-bah-HAH-thoh koh-moh har-thee-neh-roh ahl-goo-nah BESS)

Asking for References

Notice that the question about contacting "her" is exactly the same question about contacting "you," when you are speaking to a female. Likewise, the question about "him" is the same as the one about "you" when you are speaking to a male.

Can you give me a reference?	**¿Me puede dar una referencia?**
	(meh PWEH-theh dahr oo-nah reh-feh-REN-s'yah)
How can I contact her/you?	**¿Cómo la puedo contactar?**
	(KOH-moh lah PWEH-thoh kohn-tahk-TAHR)
How can I contact him/you?	**¿Cómo lo puedo contactar?**
	(KOH-moh loh PWEH-thoh kohn-tahk-TAHR)

Hiring an Employee

Following are some basic phrases that will help you establish a relationship with a new employee.

You're hired. (to a female)	**Usted está contratada.**
	(oo-STED eh-STAH kohn-trah-TAH-thah)

You're hired. (to a male)	**Usted está contratado.**
	(oo-STED eh-STAH
	kohn-trah-TAH-thoh)
You're hired. (to a group)	**Ustedes están contratados.**
	(oo-STEH-thehs eh-STAHN
	kohn-trah-TAH-thohs)

Scheduling

Following are phrases that will help you establish days and hours of work. To substitute different days and times, find the suitable words on the previous pages.

Can you come . . .	**¿Puede venir...**
	(PWEH-theh beh-NEER)
every day?	**todos los días?**
	(TOH-thohs lohs DEE-ahs)
every week?	**cada semana?**
	(KAH-thah seh-MAH-nah)
from Monday through Friday?	**de lunes a viernes?**
	(de LOO-ness ah B'YEHR-ness)
once a week?	**una vez a la semana?**
	(oo-nah BESS ah lah
	seh-MAH-nah)
on Mondays?	**los lunes?**
	(lohs LOO-ness)
twice a week?	**dos veces a la semana?**
	(DOHS BEH-sess ah lah
	seh-MAH-nah)
once a month?	**una vez al mes?**
	(oo-nah BESS ahl MESS)

twice a month?	**dos veces al mes?**
	(DOHS BEH-sess ahl MESS)
four hours a day?	**cuatro horas al día?**
	(K'WAH-troh OH-rahs ahl
	DEE-ah)
thirty hours a week?	**treinta horas a la semana?**
	(TRAYN-tah OH-rahs ah lah
	seh-MAH-nah)

Discussing Salary and Using Numbers 40+

It's important to establish how you will pay your employee right at the beginning. Review the numbers between one and thirty-one on page 121. Higher numbers are introduced below.

Your wages will be . . .	**Su sueldo será...**
	(soo SWELL-doh seh-RAH)
ten dollars an hour	**diez dólares por hora**
	(D'YES DOH-lah-ress por
	OH-rah)
twenty dollars for two hours	**veinte dólares por dos horas**
	(BAYN-teh DOH-lah-ress por
	DOHS OH-rahs)
forty-five	**cuarenta y cinco**
	(k'wah-REN-tah ee SEENG-koh)
fifty	**cincuenta**
	(seeng-K'WEN-tah)
sixty	**sesenta**
	(seh-SEN-tah)
seventy	**setenta**
	(seh-TEN-tah)

eighty	**ochenta**
	(oh-CHEN-tah)
ninety	**noventa**
	(noh-BEN-tah)
one hundred	**cien**
	(S'YEN)
one hundred and fifty	**ciento cincuenta**
	(S'YEN-toh seeng-K'WEN-tah)
two hundred	**doscientos**
	(dohs-YEN-tohs)
three hundred	**trescientos**
	(tress-YEN-tohs)
four hundred	**cuatrocientos**
	(k'wah-troh-S'YEN-tohs)
five hundred	**quinientos**
	(keen-YEN-tohs)
six hundred	**seiscientos**
	(say-S'YEN-tohs)
seven hundred	**setecientos**
	(seh-teh-S'YEN-tohs)
eight hundred	**ochocientos**
	(oh-choh-S'YEN-tohs)
nine hundred	**novecientos**
	(noh-beh-S'YEN-tohs)
one thousand	**mil**
	(MEEL)
two thousand	**dos mil**
	(DOHS MEEL)

You may have noticed that the numbers sixteen to nineteen are each written as one word (**dieciséis**, **diecisiete**, etc.) even though their literal meaning is "ten and six," "ten and seven," etc. The same is true for the numbers twenty-one to twenty-nine: **veintiuno** ("twenty and one"), **veintidós** ("twenty and two"), etc. Beginning with the thirties, and up to ninety-nine, similar combinations are written as three words:

thirty-one	**treinta y uno**
	(TRAYN-tah ee oo-noh)
forty-two	**cuarenta y dos**
	(k'wah-REN-tah ee DOHS)
fifty-three	**cincuenta y tres**
	(seeng-K'WEN-tah ee TRESS)
sixty-four	**sesenta y cuatro**
	(seh-SEN-tah ee K'WAH-troh)
seventy-five	**setenta y cinco**
	(seh-TEN-tah ee SEENG-koh)
eighty-six	**ochenta y seis**
	(oh-CHEN-tah ee SACE)
ninety-seven	**noventa y nueve**
	(noh-BEN-tah ee N'WEH-beh)

The **y** (*and*) is important in these combinations. In contrast, while we often use *and* with hundreds in English, **y** is never used with hundreds in Spanish:

one hundred (and) ten	**ciento diez**
	(S'YEN-toh D'YESS)
four hundred (and) sixty	**cuatrocientos sesenta**
	(K'WAH-troh-S'YEN-tohs seh-SEN-tah)
five hundred (and) seventy-five	**quinientos setenta y cinco**
	(keen-YEN-tohs seh-TEN-tah ee
	SEENG-koh)

Rates of Payment

The following phrases tell how to express "per" a period of time.

per hour	**por hora**
	(por OH-rah)
per day	**por día**
	(por DEE-ah)
per week	**por semana**
	(por seh-MAH-nah)
per month	**por mes**
	(por MESS)
for the completed job	**por el trabajo completado**
	(por el trah-BAH-hoh
	kohm-pleh-TAH-thoh)

Discussing Pay Periods

Make this clear at the beginning to avoid misunderstandings.

I'll pay you . . .	**Le pagaré...**
	(leh pah-gah-REH)
at the end of each day	**al fin de cada día**
	(ahl FEEN deh KAH-thah DEE-ah)
at the end of the week	**al fin de la semana**
	(ahl FEEN deh lah se-MAH-nah)
when you finish the job	**cuando termine el trabajo**
	(K'WAHN-doh tehr-MEE-neh el
	trah-BAH-hoh)
by check	**con cheque**
	(kohn CHEH-keh)
in cash	**en efectivo**
	(en eh-fek-TEE-boh)

I cannot pay you . . .	**No le puedo pagar...**
	(NOH leh PWEH-thoh pah-GAHR)
in advance	**por adelantado**
	(por ah-theh-lahn-TAH-thoh)
before the job is finished	**antes que se termine el trabajo**
	(AHN-tehs keh seh tehr-MEE-neh el tra-BAH-hoh)

Discussing Taxes

The phrases in this section will help you make it clear whether you wish to pay your employee's taxes or if you expect him to pay his own.

I will pay your Social Security taxes.	**Yo pagaré sus impuestos de Seguridad Social.**
	(YOH pah-gah-REH soos eem-pweh-stohs deh seh-goo-ree-THAD soh-S'YAHL)
You must pay your own Social Security taxes.	**Usted debe pagar sus propios impuestos de Seguridad Social.**
	(oo-STED deh-beh pah-GAHR soos PROH-p'yohs eem-PWEH-stohs deh seh-goo-ree-THAD soh-S'YAHL)
You must pay your own income taxes.	**Usted debe pagar los impuestos por sus ingresos.**
	(oo-STED deh-beh pah-GAHR lohs eem-PWEH-stohs por soos een-GREH-sohs)

I will help you with the documents.

Yo lo ayudaré con los documentos.
(YOH loh ah-yoo-thah-REH kohn lohs doh-koo-MEN-tohs)

I cannot help you with the documents.

No puedo ayudarlo con los documentos.
(NOH PWEH-thoh ah-yoo-DAHR-loh kohn lohs doh-koo-MEN-tohs)

Showing Appreciation for Good Work

These are the phrases everyone likes to hear.

You did a good job.

Ha hecho buen trabajo.
(ah EH-choh B'WEN trah-BAH-hoh)

You did a great job.

Hizo el trabajo muy bien.
(EE-soh el trah-BAH-hoh M'WEE B'YEN)

You are punctual.

Usted es muy puntual.
(oo-STED ess m'wee poon-TWAHL)

I'm happy with your work.

Me gusta su trabajo.
(meh GOO-stah soo trah-BAH-hoh)

I'm raising your salary.

Voy a aumentar su sueldo.
(boy ah ah'oo-men-TAHR soo SWELL-doh)

I am paying you extra today.

Hoy le doy algo extra.
(OY leh doy ahl-goh EK-strah)

Clearing Up Confusion

Be sure to tell your employees what to do if they have a problem or an emergency situation.

Call me if you cannot come.	**Llámeme si no puede venir.**
	(YAH-meh-meh see noh PWEH-theh beh-NEER)
In an emergency, call me.	**Si hay una emergencia, llámeme.**
	(see EYE oo-nah eh-mehr-HEN-s'yah YAH-meh-meh)
My telephone number is: 202-769-5416	**Mi teléfono es: dos cero dos, siete seis nueve, cinco cuatro uno seis.**
	(mee teh-LEH-foh-noh ess DOHS SEH-roh DOHS, S'YEH-teh SACE N'WEH-beh, SEENG-koh K'WAH-troh oo-noh SACE)
Tell me if you have a problem.	**Dígame si tiene algún problema.**
	(DEE-gah-meh see T'YEH-neh ahl-goon proh-BLEH-mah)
Tell me if you do not understand.	**Dígame si no entiende.**
	(DEE-gah-meh see NOH en-T'YEN-deh)

Terminating an Employee

These are the words nobody wants to hear, but sometimes they are necessary.

I no longer need you. (to a male)	**Ya no lo necesito.**
	(YAH noh loh neh-seh-SEE-toh)

I no longer need you. (to a female)	**Ya no la necesito.**
	(YAH noh lah neh-seh-SEE-toh)
You are fired. (to a male)	**Usted está despedido.**
	(oo-STED eh-STAH dess-peh-THEE-thoh)
You are fired. (to a female)	**Usted está despedida.**
	(oo-STED eh-STAH dess-peh-THEE-thah)
Because . . .	**Porque...**
	(POR-keh)
you didn't do the job well.	**no hizo bien el trabajo.**
	(NOH EE-soh B'YEN el trah-BAH-hoh)
you didn't come when I expected you.	**no vino cuando yo la (lo) esperaba.**
	(NOH BEE-noh k'wahn-doh yoh lah [loh] eh-speh-RAH-bah)
you never came on time.	**nunca llegó a tiempo.**
	(NOONG-kah yeh-GOH ah T'YEM-poh)
you work too slowly.	**trabaja muy lento.**
	(trah-BAH-hah m'wee LEN-toh)
you don't have the necessary skills.	**no tiene las habilidades necesarias.**
	(NOH T'YEH-neh lahs ah-beel-ee-THAH-thess neh-seh-SAHR-yahs)
you didn't follow instructions.	**no siguió las instrucciones.**
	(NOH see-G'YOH lahs een-strook-S'YOH-ness)

you don't get along with anybody.	**no se lleva bien con nadie.** (NOH seh YEH-bah B'YEN kohn NAH-th'yeh).
you have a bad attitude.	**tiene mala actitud.** (T'YEH-neh MAH-lah ahk-tee-TOOD)

Basic Questions and Answers

In this section you will learn how to form *yes-or-no* questions as well as those that begin with question words like *who, where, when,* etc. Typical answers are also provided.

Yes-or-No *Questions*

A *yes-or-no* (**sí o no**) question in Spanish is made by pronouncing a statement as a question. For example:

End a statement on the same tone you began on.

You have the money.	**Tiene el dinero.** (T'YEH-neh el dee-NEH-roh)

End a question on a tone higher than the one you began on.

Do you have the money?	**¿Tiene el dinero?** (T'YEH-neh el dee-NEH-roh)

It would be especially polite to include the person's name in answering this type of question:

Yes, Carlos.	**Sí, Carlos.**
	(SEE, KAHR-lohs)
No, Juan.	**No, Juan.**
	(NOH, H'WAHN)
Maybe.	**Quizás.**
	(kee-SAHS)
It depends.	**Depende.**
	(de-PEN-deh)
God willing!	**¡Ojalá!**
	(oh-ha-LAH)

Information Questions

The following general questions and possible answers are included to help you request or provide information.

Who . . . ?	**¿Quién?**
	(K'YEN)
I	**yo**
	(YOH)
you	**usted**
	(oo-STED)
he	**él**
	(el)
she	**ella**
	(EH-yah)
we (in a mixed or all-male combination)	**nosotros** (noh-SOH-trohs)
we (when both or all are female)	**nosotras** (noh-SOH-trahs)

27

you all	**ustedes**
	(oo-STEH-thehs)
they	**ellos**
	(EH-yohs)
they	**ellas**
	(EH-yahs)
Who with?	**¿Con quién?**
	(kohn K'YEN)
with me	**conmigo**
	(kohn-MEE-goh)
with <u>you</u>	**con <u>usted</u>**
	(kohn oo-STED)
him	**él**
	(el)
her	**ella**
	(EH-yah)
them	**ellos**
	(EH-yohs)
Whose is it?	**¿De quién es?**
	(deh K'YEN ess)
It's mine.	**Es mío.**
	(ess MEE-oh)
It's yours / his / hers / theirs.	**Es suyo.**
	(ess SOO-yoh)
What is it?	**¿Qué es?**
	(KEH ess)
It's <u>this</u>.	**Es <u>esto</u>.**
	(ess EH-stoh)

that	**eso**
	(EH-soh)
Where is it?	**¿Dónde está?**
	(DOHN-deh eh-STAH)
It's <u>here</u>.	**Está aquí.**
	(eh-STAH ah-KEE)
there	**ahí**
	(ah-EE)
over there	**allí**
	(ah-YEE)
Where are you going?	**¿Adónde va?**
	(ah-THOHN-deh bah)
I'm going <u>home</u>.	**Voy <u>a casa</u>.**
	(BOY ah KAH-sah)
to the nursery	**al vivero**
	(ahl bee-BEH-roh)
When . . . ?	**¿Cuándo?**
	(K'WAHN-doh)
now	**ahora**
	(ah-OH-rah)
later	**más tarde**
	(MAHS TAHR-deh)
soon	**pronto**
	(PROHN-toh)
always	**siempre**
	(S'YEM-preh)
never	**nunca**
	(NOONG-kah)

Until when?	**¿Hasta cuándo?**
	(ah-stah K'WAHN-doh)
Until <u>Monday</u>.	**Hasta el lunes.**
	(ah-stah el LOO-ness)
Until <u>three o'clock</u>.	**Hasta las tres.**
	(ah-stah lahs TRESS)
How . . . ?	**¿Cómo?**
	(KOH-moh)
Like this / like that	**Así**
	(ah-SEE)
For how long?	**¿Por cuánto tiempo?**
	(por K'WAHN-toh T'YEM-poh)
For <u>two hours</u>.	**Por dos horas.**
	(por dohs OH-rahs)
A few minutes.	**Unos pocos minutos.**
	(oo-nohs poh-kohs mee-NOO-tohs)
How many are there?	**¿Cuántos hay?**
	(K'WAHN-tohs EYE)
There is one.	**Hay <u>uno</u>.**
	(eye OO-noh)
There are <u>two</u>.	**Hay <u>dos</u>.**
	(eye DOHS)
There are <u>a lot</u>.	**Hay <u>muchos</u>.**
	(eye MOO-chohs)
a few	**unos pocos**
	(oo-nohs POH-kohs)

How much is it?	**¿Cuánto es?**
	(K'WAHN-toh ess)
It's twenty dollars.	**Son veinte dólares.**
	(sohn BAYN-teh DOH-lah-ress)
It's a <u>lot</u>.	**Es <u>mucho</u>.**
	(ess-MOO-choh)
only a little	**muy poco**
	(m'wee poh-koh)

Chapter 2

Establishing Policies

Your prospective employees will want to know what kinds of projects you do. These phrases will help you explain.

Introducing Your Business and Policies

This is a <u>large company</u>.

Ésta es una <u>compañía grande</u>.
(EH-stah es oo-nah kohm-pahn-YEE-ah
GRAHN-deh)

   small business

     negocio pequeño
     (neh-GOHS-yoh
      peh-KEHN-yoh)

We do <u>new</u> projects.

Hacemos proyectos <u>nuevos</u>.
(ah-SEH-mohs proh-yek-tohs
NWEH-bohs)

   outdoor

     afuera
     (ah-F'WEH-rah)

   commercial

     comerciales
     (koh-mehrs-YAH-less)

government	**para el gobierno**
	(pah-rah el gohb-YEHR-noh)
private	**particulares**
	(par-tee-koo-LAHR-ess)

We maintain <u>established areas</u>. **Mantenemos <u>áreas ya establecidas</u>.**
(mahn-teh-NEH-mohs AH-re-ahs yah
es-tah-bleh-SEE-thahs)

community parks	**parques públicos**
	(PAHR-kess POO-blee-kohs)
public streets	**calles públicas**
	(KAH-yes POOB-lee-kahs)
roads	**caminos**
	(kah-MEE-nohs)
highways	**carreteras**
	(kahr-reh-TEH-rahs)
golf courses	**canchas de golf**
	(KAHN-chahs deh GOLF)
swimming pools	**piscinas / albercas**
	(pee-SEE-nahs) (ahl-BEHR-kahs)
playgrounds	**parques de recreo para niños**
	(PAHR-kess deh reh-KREH-oh
	pah-rah NEEN-yohs)

the grounds of <u>townhouses</u>. **los jardines de <u>townhouses</u>**
(lohs har-DEE-ness deh
TOWN-houses)

apartments and condominiums **de departamentos y
condominios**
(deh deh-par-tah-MEN-tohs ee
kohn-doh-MEEN-yohs)

individual homes	**de casas particulares**
	(deh KAH-sahs par-tee-koo-
	LAH-ress)
schools	**de escuelas**
	(deh eh-SKWEH-lahs)
office buildings	**de edificios públicos**
	(deh eh-thee-FEESE-yohs
	POOB-lee-kohs)
country clubs	**de clubs privados**
	(deh KLOOBS pree-BAH-thohs)
shopping centers	**de centros comerciales**
	(deh SEN-trohs
	koh-mehrs-YAH-less)

Indicating Location of Work

These expressions will help you indicate exactly where the project will take place.

The job is <u>in / at</u> _____	**El trabajo es <u>en</u>** _____
	(el trah-BAH-hoh es en)
nearby.	**cerca de aquí.**
	(SEHR-kah deh ah-KEE)
far away from <u>here</u>.	**lejos de aquí.**
	(LEH-hohs deh ah-KEE)
the city.	**la ciudad.**
	(lah s'yoo-THAD)
a small town.	**un pueblo.**
	(oon PWEH-bloh)
the country.	**el campo.**
	(el KAHM-poh)

the suburbs.	**las afueras de la ciudad.** (lahs ah-FWEH-rahs deh lah s'yoo-THAD)

Equipment and Supplies

The following phrases will explain what equipment and supplies you will provide.

I will provide <u>the equipment</u>.	**Yo proporciono <u>el equipo</u>.** (YOH proh-por-s'yoh-noh el eh-KEE-poh)
the tools	**las herramientas** (lahs ehr-rahm-YEN-tahs)
the supplies	**los productos** (lohs proh-THOOK-tohs)
your beeper	**su biper** (soo BEE-pehr)
safety protection	**protección de seguridad** (proh-teks-YOHN deh seh-goo-ree-THAD)
first aid	**primeros auxilios** (pree-MEH-rohs ah'ook-SEEL-yohs)
Please wear <u>gloves</u>.	**Por favor use <u>guantes</u>.** (por fah-BOR OO-seh GWAHN-tess)
leather gloves	**guantes de cuero** (GWAHN-tess deh KWEH-roh)
long pants	**pantalones largos** (pahn-tah-LOH-ness LAHR-gohs)

a coat	**un abrigo**
	(oon ah-BREE-goh)
boots	**botas**
	(BOH-tahs)
steel-toe boots	**botas con punta de hierro**
	(BOH-tahs kohn POON-tah deh YEHR-roh)
heavy shoes	**zapatos gruesos**
	(sah-PAH-tohs groo'EH-sohs)
a sun hat	**un sombrero para el sol**
	(oon sohm-BREH-roh pah-rah el SOHL)
sunglasses	**lentes de sol**
	(LEN-tehs deh SOHL)
sunscreen	**bloqueador solar**
	(bloh-keh-ah-THOR soh-LAHR)
insect repellant	**repelente para insectos**
	(reh-peh-LEN-teh pah-rah een-SEK-tohs)

Explaining Emergency Policies

Your employees will appreciate knowing in advance what will happen if they should get hurt. Following are phrases that will help explain what you do when there is an accident.

If you get hurt . . .	**Si usted se lastima...**
	(see oo-STED seh lah-STEE-mah)
have an accident . . .	**tiene un accidente...**
	(t'yeh-neh oon ahk-see-THEN-teh)

get sick . . .

se enferma...
(seh en-FEHR-mah)

need assistance . . .

necesita ayuda...
(neh-seh-SEE-tah ah-YOO-thah)

tell the nearest worker

**dígaselo al obrero más
   cercano**
(DEE-gah-seh-loh ahl oh-BREH-
   roh MAHS sehr-KAH-noh)

call me

llámeme
(YAH-meh-meh)

We will <u>give you first aid.</u>

<u>**Le administraremos primeros
   auxilios.**</u>
(leh ahd-meen-ees-trah-reh-mohs
   pree-mehr-ohs ah'ook-SEEL-yohs)

take you to the hospital

lo llevaremos al hospital
(loh yeh-bah-REH-mohs ahl
   ohs-pee-TAHL)

call an ambulance

**llamaremos por una
   ambulancia**
(yah-mah-REH-mohs por oo-
   nah ahm-boo-LANS-yah)

call your family

llamaremos a su familia
(yah-mah-REH-mohs ah soo
   fah-MEEL-yah)

Selecting Employees

The following phrases will help you select the kind of workers you
need.

Establishing Policies

I need skilled workers.	Necesito **trabajadores capacitados.**
	(neh-seh-SEE-toh trah-bah-hah-THOR-ess kah-pah-see-TAH-thohs)
bricklayers	**albañiles**
	(ahl-bahn-YEE-lehs)
pipe layers	**instaladores de tuberías**
	(een-stah-lah-THOR-ess deh too-behr-EE-ahs)
irrigation experts	**expertos en irrigación**
	(ek-SPEHR-tohs en eer-ree-gahs-YOHN)
gardeners	**jardineros**
	(har-dee-NEH-rohs)
I have work for unskilled laborers . . .	**Tengo trabajo para obreros sin especialización para...**
	(TENG-goh trah-BAH-hoh pah-rah oh-BREH-rohs seen eh-speh-s'yah-lee-sah-S'YOHN pah-rah)
heavy lifting	**levantar objetos pesados**
	(pah-rah leh-ban-TAHR ohb-HEH-tohs peh-SAH-thohs)
digging	**excavar**
	(eks-kah-BAHR)
clearing brush	**sacar la maleza**
	(sah-KAHR lah mah-LEH-sah)
mowing	**cortar el cesped**
	(cor-TAHR el SESS-ped)
cleaning up	**limpiar**
	(leem-P'YAHR)

39

various jobs	**hacer varios trabajos**
	(ah-SEHR BAHR-yohs
	trah-BAH-hohs)

Explaining the Work Schedule

How long should a job, task, or project last? Or how long do you want someone to wait before doing something else? Use the following expressions to explain.

This job will last . . .	**Este trabajo durará...**
	(ESS-teh trah-BAH-hoh doo-rah-RAH)
project	**proyecto**
	(proh-YEK-toh)
task / chore	**tarea**
	(tah-REH-ah)
all day	**todo el día**
	(toh-thoh el DEE-ah)
for a short time	**un tiempo corto**
	(oon T'YEM-poh KOR-toh)
long	**largo**
	(LAHR-goh)
for five minutes	**cinco minutos**
	(SEENG-koh mee-NOO-tohs)
for an hour	**una hora**
	(OO-nah OR-ah)
for two hours	**dos horas**
	(DOHS OR-ahs)
for a week	**una semana**
	(OO-nah seh-MAH-nah)

for a month	**un mes**
	(OON MESS)
for (more than) a year	**(más de) un año**
	([MAHS deh] OON AHN-yoh)

Planning the Day

These phrases will help you tell your employees where to be, and at what time. They will also help you tell them what to do about meals and breaks during the day.

I will meet you <u>here</u>.	**Nos encontramos <u>aquí</u>.**
	(nohs en-kon-TRAH-mohs ah-KEE)
I will pick you up <u>here</u>.	**Lo recojo <u>aquí</u>.**
	(loh reh-KOH-hoh ah-KEE)
at the bus stop	**en la parada de autobuses**
	(en lah pah-RAH-thah deh ah'oo-toh-BOO-sess)
at the train station	**en la estación de trenes**
	(en lah eh-stah-S'YOHN deh TREH-ness)
on the corner	**en la esquina**
	(en lah eh-SKEE-nah)
in the parking lot	**en el parqueo**
	(en el pahr-KEH-oh)
Be here at six A.M. tomorrow.	**Esté usted aquí mañana a las seis de la mañana.**
	(eh-STEH oo-sted ah-KEE mahn-yah-nah ah lahs SACE deh lah mahn-YAH-nah)

41

You will have a twenty-minute break at 9:30.

Tendrá un descanso de veinte minutos a las nueve y media.
(ten-DRAH oon dess-KAHN-soh deh BAYN-teh mee-NOO-tohs ah las N'WEH-beh ee MEH-th'yah)

You have a one-hour break for lunch.

Tendrá una hora para almorzar.
(ten-DRAH OO-nah OR-ah pah-rah ahl-mor-SAHR)

a half-hour

media hora
(MEH-th'yah OH-rah)

You can buy your lunch nearby.

Puede comprar su almuerzo cerca del sitio de trabajo.
(PWEH-theh kohm-PRAHR soo ahl-M'WEHR-soh SEHR-kah del SEET-yoh deh trah-BAH-hoh)

soft drinks

refrescos
(reh-FRESS-kohs)

coffee

café
(kah-FEH)

Bring your own lunch.

Traiga su propio almuerzo.
(TRY-gah soo PROH-p'yoh ahl-M'WEHR-soh)

The restrooms are here.

Los baños están aquí.
(lohs BAHN-yohs eh-STAHN ah-KEE)

over there

allí
(ah-YEE)

inside

adentro
(ah-THEN-troh)

We will come back here at 4:30.	**Regresaremos aquí a las cuatro y media.**
	(reh-greh-sah-REH-mohs ah-KEE ah lahs KWAH-troh ee MEH-th'yah)
You may leave at 5:00.	**Usted puede irse a las cinco.**
	(oo-STED pweh-the EER-seh ah lahs SEENG-koh)
I'll see you tomorrow.	**Hasta mañana.**
	(AH-stah mahn-YAH-nah)
Same time, same place.	**A la misma hora, en el mismo lugar.**
	(ah lah MEEZ-mah OR-ah en el MEEZ-moh loo-GAHR)

Setting Priorities

These phrases will help you tell your employees what is important to you and to the job. Note that you insert "No" to say that something is *not* necessary or important.

This is <u>necessary</u>.	**Esto es necesario.**
	(EH-stoh ess neh-seh-SAHR-yoh)
vital	**imprescindible**
	(eem-press-een-DEE-bleh)
important	**importante**
	(eem-por-TAHN-teh)
This is <u>not necessary</u>.	**Esto no es necesario.**
	(EH-stoh NOH ess neh-seh-SAHR-yoh)
the most important	**lo más importante**
	(loh MAHS eem-por-TAHN-teh)
urgent	**urgente**
	(oor-HEN-teh)

43

Safety Precautions

Following are phrases that will help you ensure the safety of your employees and others.

Danger!	**¡Peligro!**
	(peh-LEE-groh)
Be careful!	**¡Tenga cuidado!**
	(TENG-gah kwee-THAH-thoh)
Wear <u>a hard hat</u>.	**Póngase un casco.**
	(PONG-gah-seh oon KAHS-koh)
a fall arrester	**un sistema de detención de caídas**
	(oon see-STEH-mah deh deh-ten-S'YOHN de kah-EE-thahs)
a safety belt	**un cinturón de seguridad**
	(oon seen-toor-OHN deh seh-goo-ree-THAD)
a face shield	**una máscara**
	(oo-nah MAH-skah-rah)
a dust mask	**una máscara contra el polvo**
	(oo-nah MAH-skah-rah kohn-trah el POHL-boh)
a respirator	**una filtradora del aire**
	(oo-nah feel-trah-THOR-ah del EYE-reh)
goggles	**lentes de seguridad**
	(LEN-tehs deh seh-goo-ree-THAD)

Establishing Policies

earplugs | **tapones para los oídos**
(tah-POH-ness pah-ra lohs
oh-EE-thohs)

earmuffs | **protector de oídos**
(proh-tek-TOR deh
oh-EE-thohs)

Do not drink alcohol <u>here</u>. | **No tome alcohol <u>aquí</u>.**
(NOH TOH-meh ahl-koh-OHL ah-KEE)

before coming to work | **antes de venir a trabajar**
(AHN-tess deh beh-NEER ah
trah-bah-HAR)

Do not use drugs. | **No use drogas.**
(NOH OO-seh DROH-gahs)

Smoke only during breaks. | **Fume solamente durante los
descansos.**
(FOO-meh SOH-lah-men-teh doo-
rahn-teh lohs dess-KAHN-sohs)

Chapter 3

General Instructions for Landscaping Work

n this section you will find phrases that can be applied for giving instructions in all areas of landscape work.

Giving Basic Instructions

Following are handy phrases that you can use for a variety of instructions.

I need the shovel.	**Necesito la pala.**
	(neh-seh-SEE-toh lah PAH-lah)
the tools	**las herramientas**
	(lahs ehr-rahm-YEN-tahs)
those things	**esas cosas**
	(EH-sahs KOH-sahs)
Help me.	**Ayúdeme.**
	(ah-YOO-theh-meh)
Help him.	**Ayúdelo.**
	(ah-YOO-theh-loh)

Help them.	**Ayúdelos.**
	(ah-YOO-theh-lohs)
Help us.	**Ayúdenos.**
	(ah-YOO-theh-nos)
Watch me.	**Míreme.**
	(MEE-reh-meh)
Show me.	**Muéstreme.**
	(M'WESS-treh-meh)
Tell me.	**Dígame.**
	(DEE-gah-meh)
Give me . . .	**Déme...**
	(DEH-meh)
Do it like this.	**Hágalo así.**
	(AH-gah-loh ah-SEE)
Don't do it like that.	**No lo haga así.**
	(NOH loh AH-gah ah-SEE)
Leave it like that.	**Déjelo así.**
	(DEH-heh-loh ah-SEE)

Remember that you can make many instructions negative by adding **No** at the beginning.

Use <u>this tool</u>.	**Use <u>esta herramienta</u>.**
	(OO-seh EH-stah ehr-rahm-YEN-tah)
Don't use <u>that tool</u>.	**No use <u>esa herramienta</u>.**
	(NOH OO-seh EH-sah
	ehr-rahm-YEN-tah)
this product	**este producto**
	(EH-steh proh-THOOK-toh)
Start.	**Empiece.**
	(em-P'YEH-seh)

General Instructions for Landscaping Work

Stop.	**Pare.**
	(PAH-reh)
Wait.	**Espere**.
	(eh-SPEH-reh)
Clean up.	**Limpie.**
	(LEEMP-yeh)
Take out the trash.	**Saque la basura.**
	(SAH-keh lah bah-SOO-rah)
Remove that.	**Quite eso.**
	(KEE-teh EH-soh)
Open the door.	**Abra la puerta.**
	(AH-brah lah PWEHR-tah)
Close	**Cierre**
	(S'YEHR-reh)
Turn on the water.	**Abra la llave del agua.**
	(AH-bra lah YAH-beh del AH-gwah)
Turn off the water.	**Cierre la llave del agua.**
	(S'YEHR-reh lah yah-beh del AH-gwah)
Turn on the lights.	**Encienda la luz.**
	(en-S'YEN-dah lah LOOSE)
Turn off the lights.	**Apague la luz.**
	(ah-PAH-geh lah LOOSE)
Lock up.	**Cierre con llave.**
	(S'YEHR-reh kohn lah YAH-beh)
Don't go there.	**No vaya ahí.**
	(NOH BAH-yah ah-EE)
over there	**allí**
	(ah-YEE)
to that area	**a esa área**
	(ah EH-sah AR-eh-ah)

Don't touch <u>this</u>.	**No toque <u>esto</u>.**
	(NOH TOH-keh EH-stoh)
that	**eso**
	(EH-soh)

Ask me first.	**Pregúnteme antes.**
	(preh-GOON-teh-meh AHN-tess)

Indicating Order and Repetition of Tasks

When do you want something done? And in what order? You may want something done only once, or perhaps more than once. Here are the phrases for expressing these wishes.

Do this <u>first</u>.	**Haga esto <u>primero</u>.**
	(AH-gah EH-stoh pree-MEH-roh)
after that	**luego**
	(L'WEH-goh)
at the same time	**al mismo tiempo**
	(ahl MEEZ-moh T'YEM-poh)
beforehand	**antes**
	(AHN-tess)
afterward	**después**
	(dess-P'WESS)
soon	**pronto**
	(PROHN-toh)
right away	**en seguida**
	(en segg-EE-thah)
	ahora mismo
	(ah-OR-ah MEEZ-moh)

now	**ahora**
	(ah-OR-ah)
later	**más tarde**
	(MAHS TAHR-deh)
next week	**la próxima semana**
	(lah PROHK-see-mah
	seh-MAH-nah)
at the end	**al final**
	(al fee-NAHL)

Do this <u>one time</u>.	**Haga esto <u>una vez</u>.**
	(AH-gah EH-stoh OO-nah BESS)
two times	**dos veces**
	(DOHS BEH-sess)
many times	**muchas veces**
	(MOO-chahs BEH-sess)

Indicating Location of Things

These expressions will help you tell where things are, or where they should be. Note that certain expressions end with **de**. If the word that follows is of "masculine" gender, like **camión**, **de** will change to **del**. If the word that follows is of "feminine" gender, like **casa**, **de la** is used.

It's <u>here</u>.	**Está <u>aquí</u>.**
	(eh-STAH ah-KEE)
there	**allí**
	(ah-YEE)
in front of the truck.	**delante del camión.**
	(deh-LAHN-teh del
	kahm-YOHN)

in front of the house.	**delante de la casa.**
	(deh-LAHN-teh deh lah KAH-sah)
in back of	**detrás de**
	(deh-TRASS deh)
next to	**al lado de**
	(ahl LAH-thoh deh)
on top of	**encima de**
	(en-SEE-mah deh)
under	**debajo de**
	(de-BAH-hoh deh)
across from	**enfrente de**
	(en-FREN-teh deh)
between the house and the street.	**entre la casa y la calle.**
	(en-treh lah KAH-sah ee lah KAH-yeh)
inside	**adentro**
	(ah-THEN-troh)
outside	**afuera**
	(ah-FWEH-rah)
upstairs (up there)	**arriba**
	(ahr-REE-bah)
downstairs (down there)	**abajo**
	(ah-BAH-hoh)

Driving Work Vehicles

Many landscaping jobs require driving a vehicle. In this section you will find phrases that will help you ensure that your drivers are safe, and that your instructions are carried out.

Checking for Driver's Licenses

You will want to make sure your employees have driver's licenses before they drive any vehicles. Here are some handy phrases for getting this information.

Do you have a (commercial) driver's license?	**¿Tiene usted licencia (commercial) de manejar?**
	(T'YEN-eh oo-STED lee-SENSE-yah [koh-mehr-S'YAHL] deh mah-neh-HAR)
Show me your driver's license.	**Enséñeme su licencia de manejar.**
	(en-SEN-yeh-meh soo lee-SENSE-yah deh mah-neh-HAR)
You can get a driver's license at _____.	**Se puede obtener una licencia en _____.**
	(seh pweh-the ohb-teh-NEHR oo-nah lee-SENSE-yah-en _____.)
You can get driver training at _____.	**Se pueden solicitar lecciones de manejar en _____.**
	(seh pweh-then soh-lee-see-tar leks-YOH-ness deh mah-neh-HAR en _____.)

Safe Driving

The following phrases will help you remind drivers of safety precautions, and also to give specific instructions.

Go slowly.	**Vaya despacio.**
	(BAH-yah dess-PAH-s'yoh)
faster	**más rápido**
	(MAHS RAH-pee-thoh)

53

Be alert.	**Manténgase alerta.**
	(mahn-TENG-gah-seh ah-LEHR-tah)
Do not use <u>alcohol</u>.	**No use <u>alcohol</u>.**
	(NOH OO-seh ahl-koh-OHL)
drugs	**drogas**
	(DROH-gahs)
Do not smoke while driving.	**No fume mientras maneja.**
	(NOH FOO-meh m'yen-trahs
	mah-NEH–hah)
Do not drink anything while driving.	**No tome nada mientras maneja.**
	(NOH TOH-meh NAH-thah
	m'yen-trahs mah-NEH-hah)
Concentrate 100 percent on driving.	**Ponga mucha atención al manejar.**
	(POHNG-gah moo-chah ah-tense-
	YOHN ahl-mah-neh-HAR)
Make signals.	**Haga señales.**
	(AH-gah sen-YAH-less)
Watch for underground cables.	**Ojo con los cables subterráneos.**
	(OH-hoh kohn lohs KAH-bless
	soob-tehr-RAH-neh-ohs)
In case of an accident . . .	**En caso de un accidente...**
	(en-KAH-soh deh oon
	ahk-see-THEN-teh)
stop immediately.	**pare en seguida.**
	(PAH-reh en segg-EE-thah)
turn off the engine.	**apague el motor.**
	(ah-PAH-geh el moh-TOR)
call for help.	**llame por ayuda.**
	(YAH-meh por ah-YOO-thah)

Vehicle Maintenance Instructions

These phrases explain what to do to keep a car or truck running properly.

Use <u>gasoline</u>.	**Use <u>gasolina</u>.**
	(OO-seh gah-soh-LEE-nah)
diesel fuel	**combustible diesel**
	(kohm-boo-STEE-bleh DEE-zel)
Check <u>the fuel</u>.	**Cheque <u>el combustible</u>.**
	(CHEH-keh el kohm-boose-TEE-bleh)
the oil	**el aceite**
	(el ah-SAY-teh)
Check for fuel leaks.	**Cheque si no hay una fuga de combustible**.
	(CHEH-keh see noh eye oo-nah FOO-gah deh kohm-boo-STEE-bleh)
Change <u>the oil</u>.	**Cambie <u>el aceite</u>.**
	(KAHMB-yeh el ah-SAY-teh)
the tire	**la llanta**
	(lah YAHN-tah)
the battery	**la pila**
	(lah PEE-lah)
Get <u>a jack</u>.	**Busque <u>un gato</u>.**
	(BOOSE-keh oon GAH-toh)
jumper cables	**cables para pasar corriente**
	(KAH-bless pah-rah pah-SAHR kohr-R'YEN-teh)

Giving Driving Directions

These expressions will help you tell someone how to get to another place.

Start the engine.	**Arranque el motor.**
	(ah-RAHNG-keh el moh-TOR)
Go . . .	**Vaya...**
	(BAH-yah)
Come . . .	**Venga...**
	(BENG-gah)
Drive . . .	**Maneje...**
	(mah-NEH-heh)
to the left	**a la izquierda**
	(ah lah ees-K'YEHR-thah)
to the right	**a la derecha**
	(ah lah deh-REH-chah)
straight ahead	**todo derecho**
	(TOH-thoh deh-REH-choh)
forward	**adelante**
	(ah-theh-LAHN-teh)
back	**para atrás**
	(pah-rah ah-TRAHS)
around that	**alrededor de eso**
	(ahl-reh-theh-THOR deh EH-soh)
Turn around.	**Dése una vuelta.**
	(DEH-seh oo-nah BWEL-tah)
Back up.	**Venga para atrás.**
	(BENG-gah pah-rah ah-TRAHS)

Come back. (Return.)	**Regrese.**
	(reh-GREH-seh)
Stop.	**Pare.**
	(PAH-reh)
Brake.	**Frene.**
	(FREH-neh)
Use the clutch.	**Use el cloch.**
	(OO-seh el KLOHCH)
Stop at the corner.	**Pare en la esquina.**
	(PAH-reh en lah eh-SKEE-nah)
Turn off the machine.	**Apague la máquina.**
	(ah-PAH-geh lah MAH-kee-nah)

Going Places and Taking Things

Landscaping involves a lot of moving things from one place to another. These phrases will help you give this kind of instruction. Note that *to the* . . . is **al** before certain words (those that are "masculine" in gender), and **a la** before others (those that are "feminine" in gender). If you learn the entire phrase, you won't have to worry about the gender of the word—it will come naturally.

Come here.	**Venga acá.**
	(BENG-gah ah-KAH)
Bring me the shovel.	**Tráigame la pala.**
	(TRY-gah-meh lah PAH-lah)
the hose	**la manguera**
	(lah mahng-GEH-rah)
Go . . .	**Vaya...**
	(BAH-yah)

57

Take this . . .	**Lleve esto...**
	(YEH-beh EH-stoh)
over there	**para allá**
	(pah-rah ah-YAH)
to the supervisor	**al supervisor**
	(ahl soo-pehr-bee-SOR)
to the truck	**al camión**
	(ahl kahm-YOHN)
to the job site	**al sitio de trabajo**
	(ahl SEET-yoh deh tra-BAH-hoh)
to the building	**al edificio**
	(ahl eh-thee-FEESE-yoh)
to the lumber yard	**al almacén de la madera**
	(ahl ahl-mah-SEN deh lah mah-THEH-rah)
to the dump	**al basurero**
	(ahl bah-soo-REH-roh)
to the dumpster	**al contenedor para escombros**
	ahl kohn-teh-neh-THOR pah-rah eh-SKOHM-brohs)
to the street	**a la calle**
	(ah lah KAH-yeh)
to the driveway	**a la entrada**
	(ah lah en-TRAH-thah)
to the sidewalk	**a la acera**
	(ah lah ah-SEH-rah)
to the lot	**a la parcela**
	(ah lah par-SEH-lah)

General Instructions for Landscaping Work

to the nursery	**al vivero**
	(ahl bee-BEH-roh)
to the house	**a la casa**
	(ah lah KAH-sah)
to the rock quarry	**a la cantera**
	(ah lah kan-TEH-rah)
to the hardware store	**a la ferretería**
	(ah lah fehr-reh-teh-REE-ah)
to the office	**a la oficina**
	(ah lah oh-fee-SEE-nah)
home with you	**a su casa**
	(ah soo KAH-sah)

Put that in the trash.	**Ponga eso en la basura.**
	(POHNG-gah EH-soh en lah bah-SOO-rah)
in the truck	**en el camión**
	(en el kahm-YOHN)
here	**aquí**
	(ah-KEE)
over there	**allí**
	(ah-YEE)

Chapter 4

Common Tasks for New Landscaping Projects

I f you are starting a landscaping project from scratch, or building a new structure on an existing lot, these phrases will help you give instructions.

Clearing the Lot

The following phrases enumerate the basic tasks involved in lot clearing.

Clear the brush.	**Saque las ramas.**
	(SAH-keh lahs RAH-mahs)
the trash	**la basura**
	(lah bah-SOO-rah)

Cut down the trees.	**Corte los árboles.**
	(KOR-teh lohs AHR-boh-less)
the bushes	**los arbustos**
	(lohs ahr-BOO-stohs)

Tear down the walls.	**Desmantele las paredes.**
	(dess-mahn-TEH-leh lahs pah-REH-thess)
Raze . . .	**Arrase...**
	(ahr-RAH-seh)
Break up . . .	**Rompa...**
	(ROHM-pah)
Remove . . .	**Quite...**
	(KEE-teh)
the stump	**el tocón**
	(el toh-KOHN)
the entire structure	**la estructura entera**
	(lah eh-strook-TOO-rah en-TEH-rah)
this part	**esta parte**
	(EH-stah par-teh)
Leave . . .	**Deje...**
	(DEH-heh)
that part	**esa parte**
	(EH-sah par-teh)
Replace it with fill soil.	**Reemplácelo con tierra.**
	(reh-em-PLAH-seh-loh kohn T'YEHR-rah)
Level the ground.	**Nivele la tierra.**
	(nee-BEH-leh lah T'YEHR-rah)

Grading the Lot

The following phrases refer to leveling, drainage, and retaining walls.

Remove the sod.	**Quite el césped.**
	(KEE-teh el SESS-ped)
the topsoil	**la capa superior del suelo**
	(lah KAH-pah soo-pehr-YOR del SWEH- loh)
Put it here.	**Póngala aquí.**
	(PONG-gah-lah ah-KEE)
over there	**allí**
	(ah-YEE)
Make a swale.	**Construya un canal de desvío.**
	(kohn-STROO-yah oon kah-NAHL deh dess-BEE-oh)
Build a retaining wall.	**Construya una compuerta.**
	(kohn-STROO-yah oo-nah kohm-P'WEHR-tah)
Use stone.	**Use piedra.**
	(OO-seh P'YEH-drah)
brick	**ladrillos**
	(lah-DREE-yohs)
concrete block	**bloque hueco de cemento**
	(BLOH-keh WEH-koh deh seh-MEN-toh)
railroad ties	**durmientes de ferrocarril**
	(door-M'YEN-tehs deh fehr-roh-kah-REEL)

Install the irrigation system.	**Instale el sistema de riegos.**
	(een-STAH-leh el sees-TEH-mah deh R'YEH-gohs)
Dig a hole.	**Excave un hueco.**
	(eks-KAH-beh oon WEH-koh)
a ditch	**una zanja**
	(oo-nah SAHN-hah)
a trench	**una trinchera**
	(oo-nah treen-CHEH-rah)
Install the drain pipes.	**Instale los tubos de drenaje.**
	(een-STAH-leh lohs TOO-bohs deh dreh-NAH-heh)
the drain tile	**el drenaje de barro**
	(el dreh-NAH-heh deh BAR-roh)
a diversion gutter	**un canal de desvío**
	(oon kah-NAHL deh dess-BEE-oh)
Fill it with soil.	**Llénelo con tierra.**
	(YEH-neh-loh kohn T'YEHR-rah)
gravel	**grava**
	(GRAH-bah)
rock	**piedra**
	(P'YEH-drah)
Replace the topsoil.	**Vuelva a poner la capa superior del suelo.**
	(B'WELL-bah ah poh-nehr lah kah-pah soo-pehr-YOR del SWEH-loh)
the sod	**el césped**
	(el SESS-ped)

Installing an Irrigation System

Following are instructions for installing pipes underneath the ground.

Dig <u>a trench</u>.	**Excave <u>una trinchera</u>.**
	(eks-KAH-beh oo-nah treen-CHEH-rah)
a ditch	**una zanja**
	(oo-nah SAHN-hah)
Connect <u>the pipes</u>.	**Conecte <u>las tuberías</u>.**
	(koh-NEK-teh lahs too-beh-REE-ahs)
the hose (with holes)	**la manguera (con hoyos)**
	(lah mahng-GEH-rah [kohn OH-yohs])
Place the pipes like this.	**Coloque las tuberías así.**
	(koh-LOH-keh lahs too-beh-REE-ahs ah-SEE)
Do it like this / like that.	**Hágalo así.**
	(AH-ga-loh ah-SEE)
Don't do it like that.	**No lo haga así.**
	(NOH loh AH-gah ah-SEE)
Test the system.	**Cheque el sistema.**
	(CHEH-keh el see-STEH-mah)

Tools and Equipment for Lot Preparation

Here are phrases that name typical tools and equipment for preparing a lot.

Use <u>the axe</u>.	**Use <u>el hacha</u>.**
	(OO-seh el AH-chah)
the (square) shovel	**la pala (cuadrada)**
	(lah PAH-lah kwahth-RAH-thah)
the wheelbarrow	**la carretilla**
	(lah kahr-reh-TEE-yah)
the trencher	**el trinche**
	(el TREEN-cheh)
the trackhoe	**la excavadora**
	(lah ek-skah-bah-THOR-ah)
the tractor	**el tractor**
	(el trak-TOR)
the trailer (of a truck)	**el remolque**
	(el reh-MOHL-keh)
the towtruck	**la grúa**
	(lah GROO-ah)
the truck	**el camión**
	(el kahm-YOHN)
the pickup truck	**la camioneta**
	(lah kahm-yoh-NEH-tah)
the dump truck	**el camión de volteo**
	(el kahm-YOHN deh bol-TEH-oh)
the van	**la camioneta**
	(lah kahm-yoh-NEH-tah)

Planting

In this section you will find phrases that will help you give instructions for planting. Remember that you can put the word *No* before any of these commands, to make them negative.

Soil Preparation

These phrases will help you give instructions for getting an area ready for planting.

Remove the debris.	**Saque el escombro.**
	(SAH-keh el eh-SKOHM-broh)
plaster	**los escombros de yeso**
	(lohs-eh-SKOHM-brohs deh YEH-soh)
brick	**de ladrillo**
	(deh lahth-REE-yoh)
Break up the soil.	**Desmorone la tierra.**
	(des-moh-OH-neh lah T'YEHR-rah)
Do not overcultivate.	**No la revuelva de más.**
	(NOH lah reh-BWELL-bah deh MAHS)
The clumps should be this size.	**Los terrones deben ser de este tamaño.**
	(lohs tehr-ROH-ness deh-ben sehr deh EH-steh tah-MAHN-yoh)
Add this product.	**Añada este producto.**
	(ahn-YAH-thah EH-steh proh-THOOK- toh)
fertilizer	**fertilizante**
	(fehr-tee-lee-SAHN-teh)
manure	**estiércol**
	(eh-ST'YEHR-kohl)
phosphorus	**fósforo**
	(FOHS-foh-roh)

potassium	**potasio**
	(poh-TAH-s'yoh)
lime	**cal**
	(KAHL)
sand	**arena**
	(ah-REH-nah)

Use the shovel.	**Use la pala.**
	(OO-seh lah PAH-lah)
the hoe	**el azadón**
	(el ah-sah-THOHN)
the rake	**el rastrillo**
	(el rah-STREE-yoh)
a rotary tiller	**la cultivadora rotatoria**
	(lah kool-tee-bah-THOR-ah roh-tah-TOR-yah)
the plow	**el arado**
	(el ah-RAH-thoh)
the tractor	**el tractor**
	(el trahk-TOR)

Planting Grass and Ground Cover

The following phrases will explain how to plant plugs.

Apply fertilizer.	**Aplique el fertilizante.**
	(ah-PLEE-keh el fehr-tee-lee-SAHN-teh)
Sow the seeds.	**Siembre las semillas.**
	(S'YEM-breh lahs seh-MEE-yahs)

Common Tasks for New Landscaping Projects

Use the spreader.

Use la bomba de asperjar.
(OO-seh lah BOHM-bah
deh ahs-pehr-HAR)

Plant the plugs like this.

Plante las cepas de pasto así.
(PLAHN-teh lahs SEH-pahs deh
PAH-stoh ah-SEE)

ground-cover plants

las plantas de cobertura
(lahs PLAHN-tahs deh
koh-behr-TOO-rah)

Plant them twelve inches apart.

**Plántelas a una distancia de doce
pulgadas.**
(PLAHN-teh-lahs ah oo-nah dee-
STAHN-s'yah deh DOH-seh
pool-GAH-thahs)

Laying Sod

Here are the instructions for laying sod.

Unroll the sod.

Abra el rollo de césped.
(AH-brah el ROH-yoh deh SESS-ped)

Put one strip against the next one.

Junte los rollos uno detrás del otro.
(JOON-teh lohs ROH-yohs OO-noh
deh-TRAHS del OH-troh)

Vary the seams.

Varíe las costuras.
(bah-REE-eh lahs koh-STOO-rahs)

Sprinkle with soil.

Salpique con tierra.
(sahl-PEE-keh kohn T'YEHR-rah)

Roll the sodded area.

Rode el área plantada.
(ROH-deh el AH-reh-ah plahn-
TAH-thah)

Water regularly for two weeks.

Riegue con regularidad durante dos semanas.

(R'YEH-geh kohn reh-goo-lah-ree-THAD doo-rahn-teh DOHS seh-MAH-nahs)

Do not mow yet.

Todavía no corte.

(toh-thah-BEE-ah NOH KOR-teh)

Planting Trees and Bushes

Following are phrases that will help you explain all the steps for planting trees and bushes properly.

Spread a tarp over the grass.

Ponga una lona sobre el césped.

(POHNG-gah oo-nah LOH-nah soh-breh el SESS-ped)

Dig a hole . . .

Excave un hoyo...

(ek-SKAH-beh oon OH-yoh)

big enough for roots to spread.

suficientemente grande para que se acomoden las raíces.

(soo-fee-s'yen-teh-men-teh GRAHN-deh pah-rah keh seh ah-koh-MOH-then lahs rah-EE-sess)

bigger than the burlap ball.

más grande que el cipellón.

(MAHS GRAHN-deh keh el see-peh-YOHN)

bigger than the container.

más grande que el recipiente.

(MAHS GRAHN-deh keh el reh-see- P'YEN-teh)

Common Tasks for New Landscaping Projects

deeper than the root ball.	**más hondo que el cipellón.**
	(MAHS OHN-doh keh el
	see-peh-YOHN)
Make the hole wider.	**Haga el hoyo más ancho.**
	(AH-gah el OH-yoh MAHS AHN-choh)
deeper	**más hondo**
	(MAHS OHN-doh)
Loosen the soil at the bottom of the hole.	**Suelte el suelo al fondo del hoyo.**
	(SWELL-teh el SWEH-loh ahl
	FOHN-doh del OH-yoh)
Add stones to the hole.	**Ponga piedras en el hoyo.**
	(POHNG-gah P'YEH-drahs en el
	OH-yoh)
gravel	**grava**
	(GRAH-bah)
(Do not) add organic matter.	**(No) añada materia orgánica.**
	([NOH] ahn-yah-thah mah-tehr-yah
	or-GAH-nee-kah)
Remove the binding.	**Quite el mecate.**
	(KEE-teh el meh-KAH-teh)
the burlap bag	**la bolsa que sostiene al cipellón**
	(lah-BOHL-sah keh sohs-T'YEN-eh ahl see-peh-YOHN)
the container	**el recipiente**
	(el reh-seep-YEN-teh)

Place the plant in the hole.   **Coloque la planta en el hoyo.**
                                      (koh-LOH-keh lah PLAHN-tah en el
                                          OH-yoh)

Fill the hole with the original soil. **Llene el hoyo con la tierra original**.
                                      (YEH-neh el OH-yoh kohn lah T'YEHR-
                                          rah oh-ree-hee-NAHL)

Protect the trunk with burlap.   **Proteja el tronco con tela.**
                                      (proh-TEH-hah el TROHNG-koh kohn
                                          TEH-lah)

    aluminum foil   **aluminio**
                                      (ah-loo-MEEN-yoh)

    tree-wrap paper   **papel especial para los**
                                          árboles
                                      (pah-PEL eh-speh-S'YAHL pah-
                                          rah lohs AHR boh-less)

Cover with mulch.   **Cubra con mulchin.**
                                      (KOO-brah kohn MOOL-cheeng)

    wood chips   **pedazos de madera**
                                      (peh-THAH-sohs deh
                                          mah-THEH-rah)

    pine bark   **corteza de pino**
                                      (kor-TEH-sah deh PEE-noh)

    leaf mold   **sustrato de hojas**
                                      (soo-STRAH-toh deh OH-hahs)

    peat moss   **sustrato orgánico**
                                      (soo-STRAH-toh or-GAH-
                                          nee-koh)

Common Tasks for New Landscaping Projects

Keep the mulch away from the trunk.	**Asegúrese de que el sustrato no toque el tronco.**
	(ah-seh-GOO-reh-seh deh keh el soos-TRAH-toh no TOH-keh el-TROHNG-koh)
Water well <u>once a week</u>.	**Riegue pesado <u>una vez a la semana</u>.**
	(R'YEH-geh peh-SAH-thoh oo-nah bess ah lah seh-MAH-nah)
every two weeks	**cada dos semanas**
	(kah-thah DOHS seh-MAH-nahs)
daily	**todos los días**
	(toh-thohs lohs DEE-ahs)
Put stakes around the tree.	**Ponga estacas alrededor del árbol.**
	(POHNG-gah eh-STAH-kahs ahl-reh-theh-THOR del AHR-bohl)
Tie the tree to the stake with wire.	**Apoye el árbol con la estaca.**
	(ah-POH-yeh el AHR-bohl kohn lah eh-STAH-kah)
(Do not) prune the tree.	**(No) corte las ramas del árbol.**
	([NOH] KOR-teh lahs RAH-mahs del AHR- bohl)
Cut off the <u>diseased</u> branches.	**Corte las ramas <u>enfermas</u>.**
	(KOR-teh lahs RAH-mahs en-FEHR-mahs
broken	**rotas**
	(ROH-tahs)

the young shoots on the trunk	**los brotes en el tronco**
	(lohs BROH-tess en el TROHNG-koh)

Planting Flowers, Vines, and Vegetables

Following are phrases that will help you tell your employees how to plant seeds and transplant seedlings.

Prepare the soil.	**Prepare la tierra.**
	(pre-PAH-reh lah T'YEHR-rah)
Spade the soil to a depth of eight inches.	**Cultive la tierra a una profundidad de ocho pulgadas.**
	(cool-TEE-beh lah T'YEHR-rah ah oo-nah proh-foon-dee-THAD deh OH-choh pool-GAH-thahs)
Break up the large clumps.	**Rompa los terrones.**
	(ROHM-pah lohs tehr-ROH-ness)
Remove the stones and debris.	**Saque las piedras y la basura.**
	(SAH-keh lahs P'YEH-drahs ee lah bah-SOO-rah)
Mix in organic matter.	**Añada materia orgánica.**
	(ahn-YAH-thah mah-TEHR-yah or-GAH-nee-kah)
lime	**cal**
	(KAHL)
sulfur	**azufre**
	(ah-SOO-freh)
fertilizer	**fertilizante**
	(fehr-tee-lee-SAHN-teh)

Common Tasks for New Landscaping Projects

Rake the area.	**Rastrille el área.**
	(rah-STREE-yeh el AH-reh-ah)
Get a fine texture.	**Consiga una textura fina.**
	(kohn-SEE-gah oo-nah tek-STOO-rah FEE-nah)
Make a shallow furrow.	**Haga un surco poco profundo.**
	(AH-gah oon SOOR-koh poh-koh proh-FOON-doh)
Sow the seeds <u>in a straight row</u>.	**Siembre las semillas <u>en una línea recta</u>.**
	(S'YEM-breh lahs seh-MEE-yahs en oo-nah LEEN-yah REK-tah)
evenly	**uniformemente**
	(oo-nee-for-meh-MEN-teh)
Scatter the seeds randomly.	**Salpique al voleo.**
	(sahl-PEE-keh ahl boh-LEH-oh)
Pinch the soil together after sowing.	**Pellizque la tierra después de sembrar.**
	(peh-YEES-keh lah T'YEHR-rah des-PWESS deh sem-BRAHR)
Cover the bed with a cloth.	**Cubra el arriate con un trapo.**
	(KOO-brah el ahr-YAH-teh kohn oon TRAH-poh)
Remove the weeds.	**Deshierbe.**
	(dess-YEHR-beh)
Remove the root of the weed.	**Deshierbe desde la raíz.**
	(dess-YEHR-beh des-deh lah rah-EES)
Thin the seedlings.	**Deshije las plantitas.**
	(des-EE-heh lahs plahn-TEE-tahs)

Place the seedlings four inches apart.	**Coloque las plantitas a una distancia de cuatro pulgadas.** (koh-LOH-keh lahs plahn-TEE-tahs ah oo-nah dee-STAHN-s'yah deh KWAH-troh pool-GAH-thahs)
Slip each plant into the soil.	**Ponga cada plantita en la tierra.** (POHNG-gah kah-thah plahn-TEE-tah en lah T'YEHR-rah)
Place stakes next to the tall plants.	**Coloque estacas al lado de las plantas altas.** (koh-loh-keh eh-STAH-kahs al lah-thoh deh lahs plahn-tahs AHL-tahs)
Install a trellis.	**Instale un enrejado.** (een-STAH-leh oon en-reh-HAH-thoh)
Train a vine on the trellis.	**Inicie la planta trepadora al enrejado.** (ee-NEE-s'yeh lah PLAHN-tah treh-pah-THOR-ah ahl en-reh-HAH-thoh)
Use string.	**Use mecate.** (OO-seh meh-KAH-teh)
wire	**alambre** (ah-LAHM-breh)
plastic ties	**cierres de plástico** (S'YEHR-rehs deh PLAH-stee-koh)

Planting in Containers

Following are phrases for planting in boxes and pots.

Common Tasks for New Landscaping Projects

Prepare the <u>pots</u>.

Prepare <u>las macetas</u>.
(preh-PAH-reh lahs mah-SEH-tahs)

window boxes / planters

las jardineras
(lahs har-dee-NEH-rahs)

Make sure there is a drainage hole.

Asegúrese que la maceta tenga hoyo en el fondo.
(ag-seh-GOO-reh-seh keh lah mah-SET-ah teng-gah OH-yoh en el FOHN-doh)

Place <u>pebbles</u> in the bottom.

Coloque <u>piedras</u> en el fondo.
(koh-LOH-keh P'YEH-drahs en el FOHN-doh)

pieces of broken pottery

pedazos de cerámica rota
(peh-THAH-sohs deh seh-RAH-mee-kah ROH-tah)

Add soil.

Añada tierra.
(ahn-YAH-thah T'YEHR-rah)

Place the plants one inch apart.

Coloque las plantas a una distancia de una pulgada.
(koh-LOH-keh lahs PLAHN-tahs ah oo-nah dee-STAHN-s'yah deh OO-nah pool-GAH-thah)

Add fertilizer.

Añada fertilizante.
(ahn-YAH-thah fehr-tee-lee-SAHN-teh)

Water well.

Riegue bien.
(R'YEH-geh B'YEN)

Watering

These phrases will help you explain different types of watering.

Mist gently.	**Moje suavemente.**
	(MOH-heh swah-beh-MEN-teh)
Water with a fine spray.	**Riegue con un rocío fino.**
	(R'YEH-geh kohn oon roh-SEE-oh FEE-noh)
Water the soil well.	**Riegue bien la tierra.**
	(R'YEH-geh B'YEN lah T'YEHR-rah)
Water heavily.	**Dé un riego pesado.**
	(DEH oon R'YEH-goh peh-SAH-thoh)
Use the watering can.	**Use la regadera.**
	(OO-seh-lah reh-gah-THEH-rah)
the automatic sprinkler	**el aspersor automático**
	(el ahs-pehr-SOR ah'oo-toh-MAH-tee-koh)
the hose	**la manguera**
	(lah mahng-GEH-rah)
a drip hose	**una manguera chorreando**
	(oo-nah mang-GEH-rah chor-reh-AHN-doh)
a soaker hose	**una manguera de remojo**
	(oo-nah mang-GEH-rah deh reh-MOH-hoh)
Adjust the nozzle.	**Ajuste la boquilla de salida.**
	(ah-HOO-steh lah boh-KEE-yah deh sah-LEE-thah)

Developing Outdoor Areas

Here are the phrases that will help you tell your workers how you want new outdoor building projects to be carried out.

Patios

The English word *patio* was borrowed directly from Spanish. In Spanish it is pronounced differently:

patio   **patio**
                                                   (PAHT-yoh)

You may want to remove an existing patio before building a new one. These phrases will help you with both projects.

Break up the surface.   **Rompa la superficie**.
                                                   (ROHM-pah lah soo-pehr-FEESE-yeh)

   the concrete   **el concreto**
                                                   (el kohn-KREH-toh)

Remove the bricks.   **Saque los ladrillos.**
                                                   (SAH-keh lohs lahth-REE-yohs)

   the stone   **la piedra**
                                                   (lah P'YEH-drah)

   the tile   **las baldosas**
                                                   (lahs bahl-DOH-sahs)

   the terraces   **las terrazas**
                                                   (lahs tehr-RAH-sahs)

   the high spots   **las áreas altas**
                                                   (lahs AH-reh-ahs AHL-tahs)

Fill in the low spots.

Rellene las áreas bajas.
(reh-YEH-neh lahs AH-reh-ahs
BAH-hahs)

Make the area level.

Nivele el área.
(nee-BEH-leh el AH-reh-ah)

Stake out the design.

Marque el diseño.
(MAR-keh el dee-SEN-yoh)

Excavate six inches of soil.

Excave seis pulgadas de tierra.
(ek-SKAH-beh SACE pool-gah-thahs
deh T'YEHR-rah)

Slope the area away from
the house.

**Haga un desnivel de tierra de la
casa hacia fuera.**
(AH-gah oon dess-nee-BEL deh
T'YEHR-rah deh lah KAH-sah
ah-s'yah F'WEH-rah)

Place two inches of sand in
the area.

**Ponga dos pulgadas de arena en
el área.**
(POHNG-gah DOHS pool-GAH-thahs
deh ah-REH-nah en el AH-reh-ah)

gravel

grava
(GRAH-bah)

Add concrete.

Añada concreto.
(ahn-YAH-thah kohn-KREH-toh)

aggregate

conglomerados
(kohn-gloh-meh-RAH-thohs)

pigment

pigmento
(peeg-MEN-toh)

Wait for it to harden.

Espere hasta que se endurezca.
(eh-SPEH-reh ah-stah keh seh
en-doo-RESS-kah

Common Tasks for New Landscaping Projects

Stamp the area down.	**Apisone el área.**
	(ah-pee-SOH-neh el AH-reh-ah)
Score the surface.	**Haga cortes en la superficie.**
	(AH-gah KOR-tehs en lah
	soo-pehr-FEESE-yeh)
Lay the concrete slabs.	**Coloque las piezas de concreto.**
	(koh-LOH-keh lahs P'YEH-sahs deh
	kohn-KREH-toh)
flagstone	**la loza**
	(lah LOH-sah)
slate	**la pizarra**
	(lah pee-SAHR-rah)
stone	**la piedra**
	(lah P'YEH-drah)
bricks	**los ladrillos**
	(lohs lahth-REE-yohs)
tile	**las baldosas**
	(lahs bahl-DOH-sahs)
Add mortar.	**Añada mortero.**
	(ahn-YAH-thah mor-TEH-roh)
sand	**arena**
	(ah-REH-nah)

Paths

The word for *path* in Spanish is **sendero**, and is pronounced as follows:

path   **sendero**
                                    (sen-DEH-roh)

Following are the instructions for making one.

Mark off the area, like this.	**Marque el área, así.**
	(MAR-keh el AH-reh-ah ah-SEE)
Lay a <u>sheet of plastic</u>.	**Coloque la tela de plástico.**
	(koh-LOH-keh lah TEH-lah deh
	PLAH-stee-koh)
building felt	**la felpa**
	(lah FEL-pah)
Cover with <u>wood chips</u>.	**Cubra con pedazos de madera.**
	(KOO-brah kohn peh-THAH-sohs deh
	mah-THEH-rah)
bark	**corteza**
	(kor-TEH-sah)
gravel	**grava**
	(GRAH-bah)
pebbles	**piedras pequeñas**
	(P'YEH-drahs peh-KEN-yahs)
Install <u>edging</u>.	**Instale <u>el borde</u>.**
	(een-STAH-leh el BOR-deh)
redwood 2 × 4s	**postes de madera dos por cuatro**
	(POH-stehs deh mah-THEH-rah dohs por KWAH-troh)

Ponds

A natural pond is called **laguna** in Spanish, while a man-made one is **estanque**:

Common Tasks for New Landscaping Projects

a natural pond

una laguna

(oo-nah lah-GOO-nah)

a man-made pond

un estanque

(oon eh-STAHNG-keh)

Do you want to transform a container into a small pond or pool? These phrases will help you explain how to do it.

Install an underground waterline.

Instale una tubería subterránea.

(een-STAH-leh oo-nah too-beh-REE-ah

soob-tehr-RAH-neh-ah)

a drain valve in the plastic pipe

una válvula para drenar en la tubería

(oo-nah BAHL-boo-lah

pah-rah dreh-NAR en lah

too-beh-REE-ah)

Turn off the water main.

Cierre la llave principal del agua.

(S'YEHR-reh lah YAH-beh preen-see-PAHL del AH-gwah)

Remove the existing sill cock.

Saque el grifo de manguera.

(SAH-keh el GREE-foh deh

mahng-GEH-rah)

Uncoil the plastic pipe.

Desenrolle la tubería.

(dess-en-ROH-yeh lah

too-beh-REE-ah)

Connect the valve to the pipe.

Conecte la válvula a la tubería.

(koh-NEK-teh lah BAL-boo-lah ah lah

too-beh-REE-ah)

to the sill cock

al grifo de manguera.

(ahl GREE-foh deh mahng-GEH-rah)

to the galvanized pipe **a la tubería galvanizada**
(ah lah too-beh-REE-ah
gahl-bah-nee-SAH-thah)

to the drainpipe **a los tubos de drenaje**
(ah lohs TOO-bohs deh
dreh-NAH-heh)

to the sewer / storm drain **a la alcantarilla**.
(ah lah ahl-kahn-tah-REE-yah)

Apply joint compound. **Aplique el compuesto de juntas.**
(ah-PLEE-keh el kohm-PWEH-stoh
deh HOON-tahs)

Place gravel around the valve. **Ponga grava alrededor de la**
válvula.
(PONG-gah GRAH-bah ahl-reh-theh-
thor deh lah BAHL-boo-lah)

Bury the system. **Entierre el sistema.**
(en-T'YEHR-reh el see-STEH-mah)

lower **más abajo**
(MAHS ah-BAH-hoh)

Sink the pipe in a trench. **Sumerja la tubería en un surco**
lijero.
(soo-MEHR-hah lah too-beh-REE-ah
en oon SOOR-koh lee-HEH-roh)

Test the system. **Cheque el sistema.**
(CHEH-keh el see-STEH-mah)

Turn on the water main. **Abra la llave principal del agua.**
(AH-brah lah YAH-beh preen-see-
PAHL del AH-gwah)

Common Tasks for New Landscaping Projects

Use an adjustable wrench.

Use una llave inglesa.
(OO-seh oo-nah YAH-beh eeng-GLEH-sah)

a single control valve

una válvula de control sencillo.
(oo-nah BAHL-boo-lah deh kohn-TROHL sen-SEE-yoh)

multiple

múltiple
(MOOL-tee-pleh)

an elbow connection

un conector de codo
(oon koh-nek-TOR deh KOH-thoh)

a pipe adapter

un adaptador de tuberías
(oon ah-thahp-tah-THOR deh too-beh-REE-ahs)

a threaded pipe

una tubería roscada
(oo-nah too-beh-REE-ah rohs-KAH-thah)

a sill cock assembly

un grifo de manguera
(oon GREE-foh deh mahn-GEH-rah)

a drain valve

una válvula para drenar
(oo-nah BAHL-boo-lah pah-rah dreh-NAHR)

an antisiphon valve

una válvula de antisifón
(oo-nah BAHL-boo-lah deh ahn-tee-see-FOHN)

a vacuum breaker

un interruptor de vacío
(oon een-tehr-roop-TOR deh bah-SEE-oh)

a pipe clamp	**una mordaza para tuberías**
	(oo-nah mor-DAH-sah pah-rah
	too-beh-REE-ahs)
a screw-type clamp	**una mordaza de tipo tornillo**
	(oo-nah mor-DAH-sah deh
	tee-poh tor-NEE-yoh)
a hose clamp	**una mordaza para mangueras**
	(oo-nah mor-DAH-sah pah-rah
	mahn-GEH-rahs)

Fences

A fence can be called either **un cerco** or **una cerca** in Spanish—proving that it's the <u>name</u> of something that has gender, rather than the thing itself. Following are phrases that will help you build a fence in Spanish.

Build a <u>wood</u> fence.	**Construya un cerco <u>de madera.</u>**
	(kohn-STROO-yah oon SEHR-koh deh
	mah-THEH-rah)
chain-link	**de tela metálica**
	(deh TEH-lah meh-TAH-lee-kah)
wire	**alambrado**
	(ah-lahm-BRAH-thoh)
living	**verde**
	(BEHR-deh)
a hedge	**un seto vivo**
	(oon SEH-toh BEE-boh)

Common Tasks for New Landscaping Projects

invisibile (underground, for dogs)	**invisible (subterráneo, para perros)** (een-bee-SEE-bleh [soob-tehr-RAH-neh-oh, pah-rah PEHR-rohs])
privacy	**para privacidad** (pah-rah pree-bah-see-THAD)
tall	**alto** (AHL-toh)
low	**bajo** (BAH-hoh)
four-foot tall	**a una altura de cuatro pies** (ah oo-nah ahl-TOO-rah deh KWAH-troh P'YESS)

Set the posts firmly in ground.	**Entierre los postes firmemente en la tierra.** (en-T'YEHR-reh lohs POH-stehs FEER-meh-MEN-teh en lah T'YEHR-rah)
at a distance of six feet.	**a una distancia de seis pies.** (ah oo-nah dee-STAHN-s'yah deh SACE P'YES)
in concrete.	**en concreto** (en kohn-KREH-toh)

Paint the underground part of posts with penta.	**Pinte la parte subterránea de los postes con pentanol.** (PEEN-teh lah par-teh soob-tehr-AH-neh-ah deh lohs POH-stehs kohn PEN-tah-NOHL)

Make sure the posts are straight.	**Asegúrese que los postes estén a plomo.**
	(ah-seh-GOO-reh-seh keh lohs POH-stehs eh-STEN ah PLOH-moh)
Taper the tops of the posts.	**Afile las puntas de los postes.**
	(ah-FEE-leh lahs POON-tahs deh lohs POH-stehs)
Use galvanized nails.	**Use clavos galvanizados.**
	(OO-seh KLAH-bohs gahl-bah-nee-SAH-thohs)
Join the horizontal rails at the posts.	**Junte los rieles horizontales en los postes.**
	(HOON-teh lohs R'YEH-lehs en lohs POH-stehs)
Install a gate.	**Instale una puerta.**
	(een-STAH-leh oo-nah P'WEHR-tah)
The gate should be three feet wide.	**La puerta debe ser de tres pies de ancho.**
	(lah P'WEHR-tah deh-beh sehr deh TRESS P'YES deh AHN-choh)
Attach the latches.	**Ponga los pasadores.**
	(PONG-gah lohs pah-sah-THOR-ess)
the hinges	**las bisagras**
	(lahs bee-SAH-grahs)

Chapter 5

Specific Tasks for Landscaping Maintenance

As soon as a lot is landscaped, the maintenance begins! Following are phrases that will help you explain exactly how you would like the jobs to be done.

Lawns

The vast grass lawns that surround many houses here may be a new phenomenon to your Hispanic workers, as landscaping south of the border is conceived in a very different style. You may want to explain how important the look and health of these lawns is to your clients.

Our clients care a lot about the health and beauty of their lawns.

A nuestros clientes les importa mucho que el césped esté sano y bonito.

(ah-n'wes-trohs clee-EN-tehs lehs eem-por-tah MOO-choh keh el SESS-ped eh-STEH SAH-noh ee boh-NEE-toh)

Preparing the Lawn Equipment

These phrases will help you explain the importance of working with tools and equipment that are in good working order.

Sharpen the mower blades.	**Afile las hojas de la cortadora de césped.**
	(ah-FEE-leh lahs OH-hahs deh lah kor-tah-THOR-ah deh SESS-ped)
Take the blades to be sharpened.	**Lleve las hojas a afilarse.**
	(YEH-beh lahs OH-hahs ah ah-fee-LAHR-seh)
Check the spark plugs.	**Cheque las bujías.**
	(CHEH-keh lahs boo-HEE-ahs)
Clean.	**Limpie.**
	(LEEMP-yeh)
Replace the air filter.	**Cambie el filtro.**
	(KAHM-b'yeh el FEEL-troh)
Check . . .	**Cheque...**
	(CHEH-keh)
Lubricate . . .	**Lubrique...**
	(loo-BREE-keh)
the axles	**los ejes.**
	(lohs EH-hess)
the bearings	**los baleros**
	(lohs bah-LEH-rohs)
the wheels	**las ruedas.**
	(lahs roo'EH-thahs)
Repair the wheel.	**Repare la rueda.**
	(reh-PAH-reh lah roo'EH-thah)

Specific Tasks for Landscaping Maintenance

Take the wheels to be repaired.	**Lleve las ruedas a repararse.**
	(YEH-beh lahs roo'EH-thahs ah reh-pah-RAHR-seh)
Replace the wheel.	**Póngale una rueda nueva.**
	(POHNG-gah-leh oo-nah roo'EH-thah NWEH-bah)
Check the fuel.	**Cheque el combustible.**
	(CHEH-keh el kohm-boo-STEE-bleh)
the oil	**el aceite**
	(el ah-SAY-teh)
Add fuel.	**Añada combustible.**
	(ahn-YAH-thah kom-boo-STEE-bleh)
Clean the tools.	**Limpie las herramientas.**
	(LEEMP-yeh lahs ehr-rahm-YEN-tahs)
Dry	**Seque**
	(SEH-keh)

Mowing the Lawn

Mowing the lawn is more complicated than it looks. Here are some phrases to help you explain how you want it to be done.

Use the power mower.	**Use la cortadora de motor.**
	(OO-seh lah kor-tah-THOR-ah deh moh-TOR)
push	**manual**
	(mahn-WAHL)
riding	**con asiento**
	(kohn ah-S'YEN-toh)
high-wheel	**de ruedas altas**
	(deh roo'EH-thahs AHL-tahs)

cordless	**inalámbrica**
	(een-ah-LAHM-bree-kah)
lawn tractor	**el tractor para el césped**
	(el-trahk-TOR pah-rah
	el-SESS-ped)
mulcher	**el desmenusador**
	(el des-meh-noo-sah-THOR)
grass-catcher	**que recoge la hierba cortada**
	(keh reh-KOH-heh lah YEHR-
	bah kor-TAH-thah)

Set the grass height at two inches.	**Seleccione una altura de dos pulgadas.**
	(seh-leks-YOH-neh oo-nah ahl-TOO-rah deh DOHS pool-GAH-thahs)
Cut one-third of the height of the grass.	**Corte la tercera parte de la altura del césped.**
	(KOR-teh lah tehr-SEH-rah par-teh deh lah ahl-TOO-rah del SESS-ped)
Start the mower, like this.	**Arranque la máquina, así.**
	(ah-RAHNG-keh lah MAH-kee-nah ah-SEE)
Turn off the mower, like this.	**Pare la máquina, así.**
	(PAH-reh lah MAH-kee-nah ah-SEE)
Mow the entire area.	**Corte el área entera.**
	(KOR-teh el AH-reh-ah en-TEH-rah)
Mow just this area.	**Corte sólo esta área.**
	(KOR-teh SOH-loh EH-stah AH-reh-ah)
Cut in rows.	**Corte en filas rectas.**
	(KOR-teh en FEE-lahs REK-tahs)

Specific Tasks for Landscaping Maintenance

Circle the beds.

Corte en un círculo alrededor de los arriates.

(KOR-teh en oon SEER-koo-loh ahl-reh-the-THOR deh lahs ahr-YAH-tess)

Check the bag often.

Cheque la bolsa con frecuencia.

(CHEH-keh lah BOHL-sah kohn freh-KWEN-s'yah)

Make a mulch pile.

Haga una pila de sustrato.

(AH-gah oo-nah PEE-lah deh soos-TRAH-toh)

Add the clippings to the mulch pile.

Añada lo podado a la pila de sustrato.

(ahn-YAH-thah loh poh-THAH-thoh ah lah PEE-lah deh soos-TRAH-toh)

Leave the clippings on the lawn.

Deje lo podado en el césped.

(DEH-heh loh poh-THAH-thoh en el SESS-ped)

Clean the mower blades.

Limpie las hojas de la máquina.

(LEEMP-yeh lahs OH-hahs deh lah MAH-kee-nah)

Do not back up.

No vaya al revés.

(NOH BAH-yah ahl reh-BESS)

Do not mow over the tree roots.

No corte sobre las raíces de los árboles.

(NOH KOR-teh soh-breh lahs rah-EE-sess deh lohs AR-boh-less)

Be careful near the flower beds.

Tenga cuidado cerca de los arriates.

(TENG-gah kwee-THAH-thoh SEHR-kah deh lohs ahr-YAH-tess)

Watch for rocks and debris.	**Ojo con las piedras y los escombros.**
	(OH-hoh kohn lahs P'YEH-drahs ee lohs eh-SKOHM-brohs)
Stop the mower when people approach.	**Pare la cortadora si se acerca alguna persona.**
	(PAH-reh lah kor-tah-THOR-ah see seh ah-SEHR-kah ahl-goo-nah pehr-SOH-nah)
Use the edger <u>around the flower beds</u>.	**Use el cortabordes <u>alrededor de los arriates</u>.**
	(OO-seh el kor-tah-BOR-dess ahl-reh-the-thor deh lohs ahr-YAH-tess)
at the curb	**en el borde de la banqueta**
	(en el BOR-deh deh lah bang-KEH-tah)
along the border of the lawn	**a lo largo del borde del césped**
	(ah loh LAR-goh del BOR-deh del SESS-ped)
Wear your <u>hard hat</u>.	**Póngase <u>el casco</u>.**
	(PONG-gah-seh el KAHS-koh)
ear plugs	**tapones para oídos**
	(tah-POH-ness pah-rah oh-EE-thos)
a face mask	**una máscara**
	(oo-nah MAH-skah-rah)

Aerating the Lawn

Here is the vocabulary to help you explain how to de-thatch a lawn.

De-thatch the lawn.	**Airee el césped.**
	(eye-REH-eh el SESS-ped)
Make small cuts in the soil.	**Haga cortes pequeños en la tierra.**
	(AH-gah KOR-tess peh-KEN-yohs en lah T'YEHR-rah)
Use the <u>garden fork</u>.	**Use <u>el trinche</u>.**
	(OO-seh el TREEN-cheh)
vertical mower	**la cortadora vertical**
	(lah kor-tah-THOR-ah behr-tee-KAHL)
power rake	**el rastrillo de motor**
	(el rah-STREE-yoh deh moh-TOR)
manual thatching rake	**el rastrillo de airear manual**
	(el rah-STREE-yoh deh eye-reh-AHR mahn-WAHL)
Rake up the debris.	**Rastrille los escombros.**
	(rah-STREE-yeh lohs eh-SKOHM-brohs)
Add the debris to the mulch pile.	**Añada los escombros a la pila de sustrato.**
	(ahn-YAH-thah lohs eh-SKOHM-brohs ah lah PEE-lah deh soos-TRAH-toh)

Reseeding the Lawn

You may want to tell your crew to start new grass in bare areas. Following are the phrases for this task.

Aerate the area.	**Airee la tierra del área.**
	(eye-REH-eh lah T'YEHR-rah del AH-reh-ah)
Overseed the area.	**Siembre el área.**
	(S'YEM-breh el AH-reh-ah)
Scatter the seed <u>by hand.</u>	**Siembre <u>al voleo.</u>**
	(S'YEM-breh al boh-LEH-oh)
with the mechanical spreader	**con la máquina de sembrar**
	(kohn lah MAH-kee-nah deh sem-BRAHR)
Add fertilizer.	**Añada fertilizante.**
	(ahn-YAH-thah fehr-tee-lee-SAHN-teh)
Water lightly.	**Riegue ligeramente.**
	(R'YEH-geh lee-heh-rah-MEN-teh)

Weed Control

Here is the vocabulary for explaining how to keep the lawn weed-free.

Eliminate all vegetation.	**Elimine toda la vegetación.**
	(eh-lee-MEE-neh TOH-thah lah beh-heh-tahs-YOHN)
Apply weed killer.	**Aplique el herbicida**.
	(ah-PLEE-keh el ehr-bee-SEE-thah)

Specific Tasks for Landscaping Maintenance

Be careful with the weed killer. **Tenga cuidado con la herbicida.**
(TENG-gah kwee-THAH-thoh kohn
lah ehr-bee-SEE-thah)

Start a new lawn from scratch. **Inicie un césped nuevo.**
(ee-NEES-yeh oon SESS-ped
N'WEH-boh)

Mow over the weeds. **Pase la cortadora por las hierbas
malas.**
(PAH-seh lah kor-tah-THOR-ah por
lahs YEHR-bahs MAH-lahs)

Dig out the roots by hand. **Saque las raíces a mano.**
(SAH-keh lahs rah-EE-sess ah
MAH-noh)

Use the <u>automatic</u> weed trimmer. **Use la cortadora <u>de motor</u> para las
malas hierbas.**
(OO-seh lah kor-tah-THOR-ah deh
moh-TOR pah-rah lahs MAH-lahs
YEHR-bahs)

manual **manual**
(mahn-WAHL)

Add mulch. **Añada sustrato.**
(ahn-YAH-thah soos-TRAH-toh)

Fertilizing the Lawn

You may want to explain the different types of fertilizers and where
and when you want them to be used. Following are phrases for this.

Use <u>acid</u> fertilizer here.

Use fertilizante ácido aquí.
(OO-seh fehr-tee-lee-SAHN-teh
AH-see-thoh ah-KEE)

alkaline

alcalino
(ahl-kah-LEE-noh)

Add <u>nitrogen</u>.

Añada <u>nitrógeno</u>.
(ahn-YAH-thah nee-TROH-heh-noh)

phosphorus

fósforo
(FOSS-foh-roh)

potassium

potasio
(poh-TAH-s'yoh)

<u>organic</u> fertilizer

fertilizante <u>orgánico</u>
(fehr-tee-lee-SAHN-teh
or-GAH-nee-koh)

liquid

líquido
(LEE-kee-thoh)

Use the fertilizer spreader.

Use el esparcidor de fertilizante.
(OO-seh el eh-spahr-see-THOR deh
fehr-tee-lee-SAHN-teh)

Watering the Lawn

Following are phrases for explaining how to water the grass.

Water deeply.

Dé un riego pesado.
(DEH oon R'YEH-goh peh-SAH-thoh)

Wet the soil to a depth of six inches.

Moje hasta seis pulgadas de la tierra.
(MOH-heh ah-stah SACE pool-GAH-thahs deh lah T'YEHR-rah)

Water for three hours.

Riegue durante tres horas.
(R'YEH-geh doo-rahn-teh TRESS OR-ahs)

Use the sprinkler.

Use el aspersor.
(OO-seh el ahs-pehr-SOR)

Move the sprinkler.

Mueva el aspersor.
(M'WEH-bah el ahs-pehr-SOR)

Gardens

Many people are picky about how they want their gardens cared for. These expressions will help you keep everybody happy.

Weeding Gardens

Since the types of plants cultivated in different areas are very different, you will want to point out to your workers the different types of common weeds, so that they can distinguish them from prized plants.

<u>This</u> is (not) a weed.

Ésta (no) es una mala hierba.
(EH-stah [NOH] es oo-nah MAH-lah YEHR-bah)

That

Esa
(EH-sah)

This is a flowering plant.	**Ésta es una planta que da flores.**
	(EH-stah ess oo-nah PLAHN-tah keh dah FLOH-ress)
wildflower	**una flor silvestre**
	(oo-nah FLOR seel-BESS-treh)
ground cover plant	**una planta de cobertura**
	(oo-nah PLAHN-tah deh koh-behr-TOO-rah)
vegetable	**una verdura**
	(oo-nah behr-DOO-rah)
herb	**una hierba**
	(oo-nah YEHR-bah)
perennial	**una planta perenne**
	(oo-nah PLAHN-tah peh-REH-neh)
annual	**una planta anual**
	(oo-nah PLAHN-tah ahn-WAHL)
vine	**una planta trepadora**
	(oo-nah PLAHN-tah treh-pah-THOR-ah)
bulb	**un bulbo**
	(oon BOOL-boh)

Remove all weeds of this type.	**Saque todas las malas hierbas de este tipo.**
	(SAH-keh TOH-thahs lahs MAH-lahs YEHR-bahs deh EH-steh TEE-poh)
Dig out the entire root.	**Excave la raíz entera.**
	(eks-KAH-beh lah rah-EES en-TEH-rah)

Specific Tasks for Landscaping Maintenance

Use a <u>hand spade</u>.

Use la pala de mano.
(OO-seh lah PAH-lah deh MAH-noh)

weed tool

la herramienta para malas hierbas
(lah ehr-rahm-YEN-tah pah-rah MAH-lahs YEHR-bahs)

Shake the soil from the roots.

Sacude la tierra de las raíces.
(sah-KOO-theh lah T'YEHR-rah deh lahs rah-EE-sess)

This plant is poisonous.

Esta planta es venenosa.
(EH-stah PLAHN-tah es beh-neh-NOH-sah)

Do not touch the leaves with bare skin.

No deje que las hojas toquen la piel.
(NOH DEH-heh keh lahs OH-hahs TOH-ken lah P'YELL)

This plant has thorns.

Esta planta tiene espinas.
(EH-stah PLAHN-tah T'YEH-neh eh-SPEE-nahs)

Dispose of weeds separately.

Tire las malas hierbas a la basura por separado.
(TEE-reh lahs MAH-lahs YEHR-bahs ah lah bah-SOO-rah por seh-pah-RAH-thoh)

Place the weeds in a plastic bag.

Ponga las malas hierbas en una bolsa de plástico.
(POHNG-gah lahs MAH-lahs YEHR-bahs en oo-nah bohl-sah deh PLAH-stee-koh)

Be careful not to disturb other plants.	**Cuidado de no afectar las otras plantas.**
	(kwee-THAH-thoh deh noh ah-fek-TAHR lahs oh-trahs PLAHN-tahs)
(Do not) spray these weeds with weed killer.	**(No) trate estas hierbas malas con herbicida.**
	([NOH] TRAH-teh EH-stahs YEHR-bahs MAH-lahs kohn ehr-bee-SEE-thah)
Place mulch around the plants.	**Coloque sustrato alrededor de las plantas.**
	(koh-LOH-keh soos-TRAH-toh ahl-reh-the-THOR deh lahs-PLAHN-tahs)

Keeping Gardens Active

The following expressions will help you show your employees how to deadhead flowers to encourage new blossoms, and how to harvest fresh flowers and vegetables.

Pinch off each dead blossom, like this.	**Corte las flores muertas, así.**
	(KOR-teh lahs FLOR-ess M'WEHR-tahs, ah-SEE)
Pinch off the top of the plant.	**Corte la parte superior de la planta.**
	(KOR-teh lah PAR-teh soo-pehr-YOR deh lah PLAHN-tah)
Use <u>your fingers</u>.	**Use <u>los dedos</u>.**
	(OO-seh lohs DEH-thohs)

Specific Tasks for Landscaping Maintenance

a hand pruner

tijeras de podar manuales
(tee-HEH-rahs deh poh-DAR
mahn-WAH-less)

Do not use motorized tools on
the flower gardens.

**No use herramientas de motor
en el jardín de flores.**
(NOH OO-seh ehr-rahm-YEN-tahs
deh moh-TOR en el har-THEEN deh
FLOR-ess)

Do not disturb new buds.

No afecte los capullos nuevos.
(NOH ah-FEK-teh lohs kah-POO-yohs
N'WEH-bohs)

Cut off dead flowers.

Corte las flores muertas.
(KOR-teh lahs FLOR-ess M'WEHR-tahs)

Cut off dead leaves.

Corte las hojas muertas.
(KOR-teh lahs OH-hahs M'WEHR-tahs)

Do not cut leaves of bulbs.

No corte las hojas de los bulbos.
(NOH KOR-teh lahs OH-hahs deh lohs
BOOL-bohs)

Cut leaves when they are yellow.

**Corte las hojas cuando estén
amarillas.**
(KOR-teh lahs OH-hahs kwahn-doh
eh-STEN ah-mar-EE-yahs)

Fertilize the plants.

Añada fertilizante a las plantas.
(ahn-YAH-thah fehr-tee-lee-SAHN-teh
ah lahs PLAHN-tahs)

Add two tablespoons fertilizer
to one gallon of water.

**Ponga dos cucharadas de
fertilizante en un galón de agua.**
(PONG-gah DOHS koo-chah-RAH-
thahs deh fehr-tee-lee-SAHN-teh
en oon gah-LOHN deh AH-gwah)

Sprinkle fertilizer <u>on the beds</u>.

Riegue fertilizante <u>en los arriates</u>.
(R'YEH-geh fehr-tee-lee-SAHN-teh en
lohs ahr-YAH-tes)

around the plants.

alrededor de las plantas
(ahl-reh-the-THOR deh lahs
PLAHN-tahs)

Cut the plant to the ground.

Corte la planta a raz de suelo.
(KOR-teh lah PLAHN-tah ah RAHS deh
SWEH-loh)

Pick the herbs often.

Corte las hierbas frecuentemente.
(KOR-teh lahs YEHR-bahs
freh-kwen-teh-MEN-teh)

Pick the vegetables when ripe.

**Coseche las verduras cuando estén
maduras.**
(koh-SEH-cheh lahs behr-THOO-
rahs kwahn-doh eh-STEN
mah-THOO-rahs)

Cut the flowers on a slant.

**Para cortar una flor, haga un corte
diagonal en el tallo.**
(pah-rah kor-TAR oo-nah FLOR, AH-
gah oon KOR-teh d'yah-goh-NAHL
en el TAH-yoh)

Place the cut flowers in water
right away.

**Colóque las flores en agua
en seguida.**
(koh-LOH-keh lahs FLOR-ess en AH-
gwah en segg-EE-thah)

Trees and Bushes

Your employees may not be familiar with the types of trees in your area, or with the different styles of pruning shrubs. Following are phrases that will help you explain how you wish the trees and bushes to be cared for.

Transplanting Trees and Bushes

These phrases explain how to transplant a tree or a bush.

(Do not) move this bush.	**(No) mueva este arbusto.**
	([NOH] M'WEH-bah EH-steh ar-BOO-stoh)
Dig a new hole <u>here</u>.	**Excave un hoyo nuevo <u>aquí</u>.**
	(eks-KAH-beh oon OH-yoh N'WEH-boh ah-KEE)
there	**allí**
	(ah-YEE)
Use a sharp spade.	**Use una pala bien afilada.**
	(OO-seh oo-nah PAH-lah B'YEN ah-fee-LAH-thah)
Make spade-deep cuts all around the bush.	**Haga cortes de un piquete de hondo alrededor del arbusto.**
	(AH-gah KOR-tess deh oon pee-KEH-teh deh OHN-doh ahl-reh-the-THOR del ar-BOO-stoh)
Trim off the tips of the branches.	**Corte las puntas de las ramas.**
	(KOR-teh lahs POON-tahs deh lahs RAH-mahs)

Spray with antidessicant.

Aplique un espray para que no se deshidrate.

(ah-PLEE-keh oon eh-SPRY pah-rah keh noh seh dess-eethe-RAH-teh)

Shape the roots and soil into a ball.

Haga una bola de raíces y tierra.

(AH-gah oo-nah BOH-lah deh rah-EE-sess ee T'YEHR-rah)

Cut the lower roots.

Corte las raíces más bajas.

(KOR-teh lahs rah-EE-sess MAHS BAH-hahs)

Wind burlap around the ball.

Envuelva la bola en tela.

(en-B'WELL-bah lah BOH-lah en TEH-lah)

Fasten the burlap with twine.

Sujete la tela con mecate.

(soo-HEH-teh lah TEH-lah kohn meh-KAH-teh)

Move the shrub to a shady spot.

Mueva el arbusto a la sombra.

(M'WEH-bah el ar-BOO-stoh ah lah SOHM-brah)

Spray with water.

Aspérjelo con agua.

(ah-SPEHR-heh-loh kohn AH-gwah)

Place the shrub in the planting hole.

Coloque el arbusto en el hoyo.

(koh-LOH-keh el ahr-BOO-stoh en el OH-yoh)

Remove the twine.

Quite el mecate.

(KEE-teh el meh-KAH-teh)

Fill the hole with soil.

Llene el hoyo con tierra.

(YEH-neh el OH-yoh kohn T'YEHR-rah)

Add mulch.

Añada sustrato.

(ah-YAH-thah soo-STRAH-toh)

Water well.	**Riegue bien.**
	(R'YEG-eh B'YEN)
Mist lightly every day for two weeks.	**Moje ligeramente durante <u>dos</u> semanas.**
	(MOH-heh lee-heh-rah-MEN-teh doo-rahn-teh DOHS seh-MAH-nahs)
Water <u>once</u> a week.	**Riéguelo <u>una</u> vez a la semana.**
	(R'YEG-eh-loh OO-nah BESS ah lah seh-MAH-nah)
twice	**dos veces**
	(DOHS BEH-sess)

Feeding Trees and Bushes

You will want to explain that different types of trees and bushes require different types of fertilizer. Here are some expressions for giving the best diet to your trees.

(Do not) feed this <u>tree</u>.	**(No) ponga fertilizante en este árbol.**
	([NOH] POHNG-gah fehr-tee-lee-SAHN-teh en EH-steh AHR-bohl)
bush	**arbusto**
	(ar-BOO-stoh)
Use <u>liquid</u> fertilizer.	**Use fertilizante <u>liquido</u>.**
	(OO-seh fehr-tee-lee-SAHN-teh LEE-kee-thoh)
granular	**granular**
	(grah-noo-LAHR)

107

10-10-10

diez-diez-diez
(D'YES-D'YES-D'YES)

16-4-8

dieciséis-cuatro-ocho
(d'yeh-see-SACE-KWAH-troh-
OH-choh)

Add <u>nitrogen</u>.

Añada nitrógeno.
(ahn-YAH-thah nee-TROH-heh-noh)

phosphorous

fósforo
(FOHS-foh-roh)

potassium

potasio
(poh-TAH-s'yoh)

Inject fertilizer into the soil,
like this.

**Entierre el fertilizante a la
tierra, así.**
(en-T'YEHR-reh el fehr-tee-lee-SAHN-
teh ah lah T'YEHR-rah, ah-SEE)

Broadcast fertilizer on the surface.

**Disemine el fertilizante en la
superficie.**
(dee-seh-MEE-neh el fehr-tee-lee-
SAHN-teh en lah soo-pehr-
FEE-s'yeh)

Place fertilizer under the
visible roots.

**Aplique el fertilizante debajo de
las raíces visibles.**
(ah-PLEE-keh el fehr-tee-lee-SAHN-
teh deh-BAH-hoh deh lahs rah-EE-
sess bee-SEE-bless)

Add <u>more</u> fertilizer.

Ponga <u>más</u> fertilizante.
(POHNG-gah MAHS fehr-tee-lee-
SAHN-teh)

less

menos
(MEH-nohs)

Pruning and Making Repairs

Pruning can make or break the look of a garden and affect the health of the tree or bush. The following phrases will help you do the job properly and explain your clients' wishes.

(Do not) cut off these branches.	**(No) corte estas ramas.**
	([NOH] KOR-teh EH-stahs RAH-mahs)
the <u>lower</u> branches	**las ramas <u>más bajas</u>**
	(lahs RAH-mahs MAHS BAH-hahs)
upper	**más altas**
	(MAHS AHL-tahs)
diseased	**enfermas**
	(en-FEHR-mahs)
broken	**rotas**
	(ROH-tahs)
Remove smaller branches.	**Quite las ramas más pequeñas.**
	(KEE-teh lahs RAH-mahs MAHS peh-KEN-yahs)
Cut the branches flush with the limb.	**Corte las ramas alineadas con el tronco.**
	(KOR-teh lahs RAH-mahs ah-lee-neh-AH-thahs kohn el TROHNG-koh)
Trim these branches.	**Pode estas ramas.**
	(POH-theh EH-stahs RAH-mahs)
Cut off the tips of these branches.	**Corte las puntas de estas ramas.**
	(KOR-teh lahs POON-tahs deh EH-stahs RAH-mahs)
Remove suckers at the root.	**Quite los chupones desde la raíz.**
	(KEE-teh lohs choo-POH-ness dez-deh lah rah-EES)

Thin the bush, like this.

Aclare el arbusto, así.

(ah-KLAH-reh el ar-BOO-stoh ah-SEE)

Keep the natural shape of
the bush.

**Mantenga la forma natural
del arbusto.**

(mahn-TENG-gah lah FOR-mah nah-
too-RAHL del ahr-BOO-stoh)

Trim the bush to a rounded
shape.

**Corte el arbusto en una forma
redonda.**

(KOR-teh el ahr-BOO-stoh en oo-nah
FOR-mah reh-THOHN-dah)

square

cuadrada

(kwahth-RAH-thah)

Use manual tools.

Use herramientas manuales.

(OO-seh ehr-rahm-YEN-tahs
mahn-WAH-less)

motorized

de motor

(de moh-TOR)

Use pruning shears.

Use tijeras de podar.

(OO-seh tee-HEH-rahs deh
poh-THAHR)

a saw

una sierra

(oo-nah S'YEHR-rah)

loppers / long-handled shears

tijeras de mango largo

(tee-HEH-rahs deh MANG-goh
LAHR-goh)

hedge clippers

podadoras

(poh-thah-THOR-ahs)

Paint open wounds on the trees.

Pinte las heridas de los árboles.

(PEEN-teh lahs eh-REE-thahs deh lohs
AHR-boh-less)

Remove birds' nests.

Quite los nidos de pájaros.

(KEE-teh lohs NEE-thohs deh
PAH-hah-rohs)

Patch holes made by animals.

Parche los huecos hechos por animales.

(PAHR-cheh lohs WEH-kohs eh-chohs
por lohs ah-nee-MAH-less)

Trim away dead bark.

Quite la corteza muerta.

(KEE-teh lah kor-TEH-sah
M'WEHR-tah)

Paint the affected area.

Pinte el área afectada.

(PEEN-teh el AH-reh-ah
ah-fek-TAH-thah)

Use this paint only.

Use solamente esta pintura.

(OO-seh soh-lah-men-teh EH-stah
peen-TOO-rah)

Cut off injured roots.

Corte las raíces heridas.

(KOR-teh lahs rah-EE-sess
eh-REE-thahs)

Remove <u>climbing vines</u>.

Quite <u>las plantas trepadoras</u>.

(KEE-teh lahs PLAHN-tahs
treh-pah-THOR-ahs)

the ivy

la hiedra

(lah YETH-rah)

Yard Cleanup

After all the hard work of beautifying a lawn or garden, the final step of cleaning up is important. These phrases will help you get the job done the way you like it.

Leaf Removal

Here are phrases for raking, blowing, and bagging leaves.

<u>Rake</u> these leaves into a pile.

Rastrille estas hojas en una pila.
(rah-STREE-yeh eh-stahs OH-hahs en oo-nah PEE-lah)

Blow

Sople
(SOH-pleh)

Rake carefully in the flower beds.

Rastrille con cuidado en los arriates.
(rah-STREE-yeh kohn kwee-THAH-thoh en los ahr-YAH-tess)

Add the leaves to the compost pile.

Añada las hojas a la pila de la composta.
(ahn-YAH-thah lahs OH-hahs ah lah PEE-lah deh lah kom-POH-stah)

Pile the leaves on the curb for recycling.

Ponga las hojas al borde de la banqueta para el reciclaje.
(POHNG-gah lahs OH-hahs ahl BOR-deh deh lah bahng-KEH-tah pah-rah el reh-see-KLAH-heh)

Put the leaves in these bags.

Ponga las hojas en estas bolsas.
(POHNG-gah lahs OH-hahs en eh-stahs BOHL-sahs)

Tie the bags securely.

Amarre bien las bolsas.
(ah-MAHR-reh B'YEN lahs BOHL-sahs)

Take the bags to _____.

Lleve las bolsas al _____.
(YEH-beh lahs BOHL-sahs ahl _____)

the truck

el camion
(el kahm-YOHN)

the recycling center	**el reciclaje**
	(el reh-see-KLAH-heh)
the dump	**el tiradero**
	(el tee-rah-THEH-roh)
the curb	**el borde de la banqueta**
	(el BOR-deh deh lah
	bahng-KEH-tah)

Use a rake.	**Use un rastrillo.**
	(OO-seh oon rah-STREE-yoh)
the leaf blower	**la sopladora de hojas**
	(lah soh-plah-THOR-ah deh
	OH-hahs)

Disposal of Debris

Following are phrases for removing the clippings and debris from the premises.

Cut branches into small pieces.	**Corte las ramas en pedazos pequeños.**
	(KOR-teh lahs RAH-mahs en peh-THAH-sohs peh-KEN-yos)
Rake up	**Rastrille**
	(rah-STREE-yeh)
Pick up	**Recoja**
	(reh-KOH-hah)
the pieces.	**los pedazos.**
	(lohs-peh-THAH-sohs)
the clippings	**la cortada**
	(lah kor-TAH-thah)

the debris	**los escombros**
	(lohs eh-SKOHM-brohs)
the trash	**la basura**
	(lah bah-SOO-rah)

Pile them on the truck.	**Póngalos en el camión.**
	(POHNG-gah-lohs en el kam-YOHN)
Leave them here.	**Déjelos aquí.**
	(DEH-heh-lohs ah-KEE)
Take them to the curb.	**Llévelos al borde de la banqueta.**
	(YEH-beh-lohs ahl BOR-deh deh lah
	bahng-KEH-tah)
Take it to the dump.	**Llévelo al tiradero.**
	(YEH-beh-loh ahl tee-rah-THEH-roh)

Snow Removal

In many areas, snow removal is a big part of landscape maintenance. Following are some phrases that will help you explain how you want it to be done.

Remove the snow from the <u>driveway</u>.	**Quite la nieve del '<u>driveway</u>'.**
	(KEE-teh lah N'YEH-beh
	del-DRIBE-weh-ee)
from the sidewalk	**de la acera**
	(deh lah ah-SEH-rah)
from the path	**de la vereda**
	(deh lah beh-REH-thah)
from the stoop	**de la entrada**
	(deh lah en-TRAH-thah)
from the patio	**del patio**
	(del PAHT-yoh)

Specific Tasks for Landscaping Maintenance

from the steps	**de las escaleras**
	(deh lahs eh-skah-LEH-rahs)
from the roof	**del techo**
	(del TEH-choh)
from the gutters	**de las canaletas**
	(deh lahs kah-nah-LEH-tahs)

Use a <u>snow shovel</u>.　　**Use una <u>pala para la nieve</u>.**
(OO-seh oo-nah PAH-lah pah-rah lah
　　N'YEH-beh)

snowblower　　　**una sopladora para la nieve**
　　　(oo-nah soh-plah-THOR-ah
　　　pah-rah lah N'YEH-beh)

Do not throw snow on　　**No tire la nieve encima de los**
　　the bushes.　　　**arbustos.**
(NOH TEE-reh lah N'YEH-beh en-see-
　　mah deh lohs ahr-BOO-stohs)

Remove the snow from the　　**Quite la nieve de las ramas de**
　　tree limbs.　　　**los árboles.**
(KEE-teh lah N'YEH-beh deh lahs
　　RAH-mahs deh lohs AHR-boh-less)

Remove the icicles.　　**Quite los pedazos de hielo.**
(KEE-teh lohs peh-THAH-sohs deh
　　YEH-loh)

Put <u>salt</u> on icy spots.　　**Ponga <u>sal</u> en las áreas resbalosas.**
(POHNG-gah SAHL en lahs AH-reh-
　　ahs ress-bah-LOH-sahs)

sand　　　**arena**
　　　(ah-REH-nah)

Power Washing

Now that it's available, everybody seems to want to have certain areas power-washed. Following are some phrases that give instructions for doing this in Spanish.

Power-wash the driveway.	**Limpie la entrada con agua a presión.**
	(LEEMP-yeh lah en-TRAH-thah kohn AH-gwah ah press-YOHN)
the sidewalk	**la acera**
	(lah-ah-SEH-rah)
the steps	**las escaleras**
	(lahs eh-skah-LEH-rahs)
the patio	**el patio**
	(el-PAHT-yoh)
the bricks	**los ladrillos**
	(lohs lahth-REE-yohs)
the siding	**el revestimiento**
	(el reh-beh-steem-YEN-toh)
Be careful.	**Tenga cuidado.**
	(TENG-gah kwee-THAH-thoh)
Turn off the machine if someone approaches.	**Apague la máquina si alguien se acerca.**
	(ah-PAH-geh lah MAH-kee-nah see ahl-g'yen seh ah-SEHR-kah)

Pests and Diseases

Following are phrases that will help you explain how to reduce the damage caused by insects, other animals, and plant diseases.

Collect the fallen leaves.

Recoja las hojas caídas.
(reh-KOH-hah lahs oh-hahs
kah-EE-thahs)

Burn

Queme
(KEH-meh)

Remove the weeds in the area.

Saque las malas hierbas del área.
(SAH-keh lahs MAH-lahs YEHR-bahs
del AH-reh-ah)

Hand-pick the worms.

Saque los gusanos con las manos.
(SAH-keh lohs goo-SAH-nohs kohn
lahs MAH-nohs)

cocoons

los capullos
(lohs kah-POO-yohs)

Prune the dead branches.

Corte las ramas muertas.
(KOR-teh lahs RAH-mahs
M'WEHR-tahs)

weakened

débiles
(DEH-bee-less)

Destroy the infected plant parts.

**Corte las partes infectadas de la
planta.**
(KOR-teh lahs PAR-tess een-fek-TAH-
thahs deh lah PLAHN-tah)

entire plant

la planta entera
(lah PLAHN-tah en-TEH-rah)

117

Do not add diseased plants to the compost pile.	**No añada las plantas infectadas a la pila de la composta.** (NOH ahn-YAH-thah lahs PLAHN-tahs een-fek-TAH-thahs ah lah PEE-lah deh lah kom-POH-stah)
Disinfect the shears.	**Desinfecte las tijeras de podar.** (dess-een-FEK-teh lahs tee-HEH-rahs deh poh-THAHR)
Apply fungicide.	**Aplique fungicida.** (ah-PLEE-keh foon-hee-SEE-thah)
dormant oil spray	**aspersor del aceite de dormancia** (ahs-pehr-SOR del ah-SAY-teh deh dor-MAHN-s'yah)
insecticide	**insecticida** (een-sek-tee-SEE-thah)
snail baits	**cebos para caracoles** (SEH-bohs pah-rah kah-rah-KOH-less)
slugs	**babosas** (bah-BOH-sahs)
Use spray.	**Use espray.** (OO-seh eh-SPRY)
powder	**polvo** (POHL-boh)
natural controls	**control natural** (kohn-TROHL nah-too-RAHL)
chemicals	**productos quimicos** (proh-thook-tohs KEE-mee-kohs)

Specific Tasks for Landscaping Maintenance

Place a paper collar around the stem.

Coloque un collar de papel alrededer del tallo.

(koh-LOH-keh oon koh-YAR deh pah-PELL ahl-reh-the-thor del TAH-yoh)

Wrap the trunk with tree wrap.

Envuelva el tronco con tela para árboles.

(en-B'WELL-bah el TROHNG-koh kohn TEH-lah pah-rah AHR-boh-less)

corrugated paper

papel corrugado

(pah-PELL kor-roo-GAH-thoh)

Cover the plant with netting.

Cubra la planta con malla.

(KOO-brah lah plahn-tah kohn MAH-yah)

Appendix

Numbers

0	cero	20	veinte
1	uno	21	veintiuno
2	dos	22	veintidós
3	tres	23	veintitrés
4	cuatro	24	veinticuatro
5	cinco	25	veinticinco
6	seis	26	veintiséis
7	siete	27	veintisiete
8	ocho	28	veintiocho
9	nueve	29	veintinueve
10	diez		
		30	treinta
11	once	31	treinta y uno
12	doce	32	treinta y dos
13	trece	33	treinta y tres
14	catorce	34	treinta y cuatro
15	quince	35	treinta y cinco
16	dieciseis	36	treinta y seis
17	diecisiete	37	treinta y siete
18	dieciocho	38	treinta y ocho
19	diecinueve	39	treinta y nueve

Appendix

40	cuarenta	68	sesenta y ocho
41	cuarenta y uno	69	sesenta y nueve
42	cuarenta y dos		
43	cuarenta y tres	70	setenta
44	cuarenta y cuatro	71	setenta y uno
45	cuarenta y cinco	72	setenta y dos
46	cuarenta y seis	73	setenta y tres
47	cuarenta y siete	74	setenta y cuatro
48	cuarenta y ocho	75	setenta y cinco
49	cuarenta y nueve	76	setenta y seis
		77	setenta y siete
50	cincuenta	78	setenta y ocho
51	cincuenta y uno	79	setenta y nueve
52	cincuenta y dos		
53	cincuenta y tres	80	ochenta
54	cincuenta y cuatro	81	ochenta y uno
55	cincuenta y cinco	82	ochenta y dos
56	cincuenta y seis	83	ochenta y tres
57	cincuenta y siete	84	ochenta y cuatro
58	cincuenta y ocho	85	ochenta y cinco
59	cincuenta y nueve	86	ochenta y seis
		87	ochenta y siete
60	sesenta	88	ochenta y ocho
61	sesenta y uno	89	ochenta y nueve
62	sesenta y dos		
63	sesenta y tres	90	noventa
64	sesenta y cuatro	91	noventa y uno
65	sesenta y cinco	92	noventa y dos
66	sesenta y seis	93	noventa y tres
67	sesenta y siete	94	noventa y cuatro

Numbers

95	noventa y cinco	200	doscientos
96	noventa y seis	300	trescientos
97	noventa y siete	400	cuatrocientos
98	noventa y ocho	500	quinientos
99	noventa y nueve	600	seiscientos
		700	setecientos
100	cien	800	ochocientos
101	ciento uno	900	novecientos
102	ciento dos		
114	ciento catorce	1000	mil
129	ciento veintinueve	1999	mil novecientos
133	ciento treinta y tres		noventa y nueve
142	ciento cuarenta y dos	2000	dos mil
156	ciento cincuenta y seis	2009	dos mil nueve
167	ciento sesenta y siete	40,000	cuarenta mil
179	ciento setenta y nueve		
188	ciento ochenta y ocho	1,000,000	un millón
194	ciento noventa y cuatro		

English-Spanish Glossary

Expressions

English	Spanish
A.M.	de la mañana
Be careful.	Cuidado. / Tenga cuidado.
Call 911.	Llame al nueve-uno-uno.
Don't . . .	No...
Excuse me.	Disculpe.
For how long . . .	¿Por cuánto tiempo...?
God willing.	¡Ojalá!
Good afternoon.	Buenas tardes.
Good evening.	Buenas tardes / noches.
Good morning.	Buenos días.
Good night.	Buenas noches.
Good-bye.	Adiós.
Hello.	Hola.
How are you?	¿Cómo está usted?
How do you say . . . ?	¿Cómo se dice...?
How many . . . ?	¿Cuántos...?
How much . . . ?	¿Cuánto...?
How . . . ?	¿Cómo...?
I'm sorry.	Lo siento.
in case of an emergency	en caso de una emergencia
No	No
P.M.	de la tarde, de la noche
Please.	Por favor.
See you later.	Hasta luego.
Thank you.	Gracias.
Until when . . . ?	¿Hasta cuándo...?
Welcome.	Bienvenido.
What for . . . ?	¿Para qué...?
What . . . ? (name, telephone number)	¿Cuál es..?

What . . . ? (thing)	¿Qué...?
What time is it?	¿Qué hora es?
When . . . ?	¿Cuándo...?
Where . . . ?	¿Dónde...?
Where from . . . ?	¿De dónde...?
Where to . . . ?	¿Adónde...?
Who . . . ?	¿Quién...?
Who with . . . ?	¿Con quién...?
Whose . . . ?	¿De quién...?
Why . . . ?	¿Por qué?
Yes.	Sí.
You're welcome.	De nada.

People

boss	jefe / patrón
boyfriend	novio
bricklayer	albañil
brother	hermano
child	niño, niña
children	niños, niñas
children (sons and daughters)	hijos, hijas
daughter	hija
family	familia
father	papá / padre
friend	amigo, amiga
gardener	jardinero, jardinera
girlfriend	novia
he	él
her	la, le, a ella
him	lo, le, a él
husband	esposo
I	yo
irrigation experts	expertos en irrigación
laborer	obrero
mother	mamá / madre
neighbor	vecino, vecina
nobody	nadie
parents	padres
pipe layer	instalador de tuberías
she	ella
sister	hermana
someone	alguien
son	hijo

they	ellos / ellas
we	nosotros / nosotras
wife	esposa
worker	trabajador, trabajadora
you	usted
you all	ustedes

Places

apartment	departamento, apartamento
area	área
bathroom	baño
bottom	fondo
building	edificio
bus stop	parada de autobuses
city	ciudad
corner (inside)	rincón
corner (outside)	esquina
country club	club de campo
countryside	campo
curb	banqueta
condominium	condominio
driveway	entrada / driveway
dump	tiradero / basurero
garden	jardín
golf course	cancha de golf
hardware store	ferretería
highway	carretera / autopista
hospital	hospital
house	casa
job site	sitio de trabajo
lot	parcela
lumberyard	almacén de la madera
nursery	vivero
office building	edificio público
office	oficina
path	sendero / vereda
patio	patio
playground	parque de recreo para niños
park	parque
quarry	cantera
restroom	baño
road	camino / carretera
school	escuela

shopping center	centro comercial
sidewalk	acera
street	calle
suburbs	las afueras de la ciudad
townhouse	townhouse
train station	estación de trenes

Things

accident	accidente
adapter	adaptador
aggregate	conglomerado
alcohol	alcohol
aluminum foil	aluminio
ambulance	ambulancia
animal	animal
annual	planta anual
antisiphon	antisifón
assistance	ayuda
attitude	actitud
axe	hacha
axle	eje
backhoe	excavadora
bag	bolsa
baits	cebos
ball	bola
battery	pila / batería
bearings	baleros
bed (of flowers)	arriate
beeper	biper
belt	cinturón
binding	mecate
blades	hojas
boots	botas
border	borde
branch	rama
break (rest period)	descanso
brick	ladrillo
brush (weeds)	maleza / hierba mala
bud	capullo
bulb	bulbo
bush	arbusto
business	negocio
cable	cable

cash	efectivo
check	cheque
chemicals	productos químicos
chore	tarea
circle	círculo
clamp (hose)	mordaza para mangueras
clamp (pipe)	mordaza para tuberías
clamp (screw-type)	mordaza de tipo tornillo
client	cliente
clippers	podadoras
clippings	lo podado / la cortada
cloth	trapo
clump	terrón
clutch	embriague
coat	abrigo
cocoon	capullo
coffee	café
collar	collar
community	comunidad
company	compañía
compost pile	pila de composta / sustrato
concrete block	bloque hueco de cemento
concrete	concreto
container	recipiente
control	control
danger	peligro
debris	escombro
depth	profundidad
design	diseño
diesel fuel	combustible diesel
ditch	zanja
diversion gutter	canal de desvío
documents	documentos
dollars	dólares
dormant oil spray	aspersor del aceite de dormancia
drain	drenaje
drain pipes	tubos de drenaje
drain tile	drenaje de barro
drain valve	válvula de drenaje
drink, soft	refresco
driver's license	licencia de manejar
drugs	drogas
dump truck	camión de volteo
dumpster	contenedor para escombros
dust	polvo

earmuffs	protector de oídos
earplugs	tapones para los oídos
earth	tierra
edger	cortabordes
edging	borde
elbow connection	conector de codo
emergency	emergencia
engine	motor
equipment	equipo
fabric	tela
face shield	máscara
fall	caída
felt	felpa
fence	cerco / cerca
fertilizer	fertilizante
filter	filter
finger	dedo
first aid	primeros auxilios
flagstone	loza
flower	flor
flower bed	arriate
flower pot	maceta
flowering plant	planta que da flores
fork (garden)	trinche
fuel leak	fuga de combustible
fungicide	fungicida
furrow	surco
gallon	galón
gasoline	gasolina
gate	puerta
gloves	guantes
goggles	lentes de seguridad
government	gobierno
grass catcher	recogedor de cortada
gravel	grava
ground	tierra
ground cover	plantas de cobertura
grounds	terrenos, jardines
gutters	canaletas
hard hat	casco
hat (for the sun)	sombrero
hedge	seto vivo / cerco verde
hedge clippers	podadoras
height	altura
help	ayuda
herb	hierba

hinge	bisagra
hoe	azadón
hole	hoyo / hueco
hose (drip)	manguera chorreando
hose (soaker)	manguera de remojo
icicles	pedazos de hielo
inch	pulgada
insect repellant	repelente para insectos
insecticide	insecticida
instructions	instrucciones
irrigation	irrigación / riegos
ivy	hiedra
jack	gato
job	trabajo
joint compound	compuesto de juntas
jumper cables	cables de pasar corriente
latch	pasador
lawn mower	cortadora de césped
lawn mower (high-wheel)	cortadora de ruedas altas
lawn mower (power)	cortadora de motor
lawn mower (push)	cortadora manual
lawn mower (riding)	cortadora con asiento
lawn tractor	tractor para el césped
leaf	hoja
leaf blower	sopladora de hojas
leaf mold	sustrato
lessons	lecciones
lifting	levantamiento de objetos pesados
lime	cal
liquid	líquido
loppers	tijeras de mango largo
lunch	almuerzo
machine	máquina
manure	estiércol
mask	máscara
matter	materia
minute	minuto
mold	sustrato
money	dinero
month	mes
mortar	cemento / mortero
mower	cortadora de césped
mulch	sustrato, composta, mulchin
mulcher	desmenusador
nail	clavo
name	nombre

natural	natural
nest (of bird)	nido de pájaros
netting	malla
nitrogen	nitrógeno
nozzle	boquilla de salida
oil	aceite
paint	pintar
pants	pantalones
paper	papel
part	parte
pay	sueldo
peat moss	sustrato orgánico
pebbles	piedras
perennial	planta perenne
phosphorus	fósforo
pickup truck	camioneta
piece	pedazo
pigment	pigmento
pile	pila
pine bark	corteza de pino
pipes	tuberías
place	lugar
planter	jardinera
plaster	yeso
plow	arado
plugs (of grass)	cepas de pasto
pond (man-made)	estanque
pond (natural)	laguna
pot (for flowers)	maceta
potassium	potasio
pottery	cerámica / barro
post, wooden	poste
powder	polvo
privacy	privacidad
problem	problema
product	producto
project	proyecto
protection	protección
pruners	tijeras de podar
railroad ties	durmientes de ferrocarril
raise	aumento
rake	rastrillo
recycling	reciclaje
reference	referencia
respirator	filtradora de aire
retaining wall	compuerta / dique

rock	piedra
roof	techo
root	raíz
root ball	cipellón
rotary tiller	cultivadora rotatoria
row	fila / línea
safety	seguridad
salary	sueldo
salt	sal
sand	arena
saw	sierra
seams	costuras
seedling	plantita
seeds	semillas
sewer	alcantarilla
shade	sombra
shoes	zapatos
shoots	brotes
shovel (snow)	pala para la nieve
shovel	pala
signals	señales
sill cock	grifo de manguera
skills	habilidades
skin	piel
slabs	piezas
slate	pizarra
slope	desnivel
slug	babosa
snail	caracol
snow	nieve
snow shovel	pala para la nieve
snowblower	sopladora para la nieve
sod	césped
soft drink	refresco
soil	tierra
spade	pala
spade (hand)	pala de mano
spark plugs	bujías
spray (aerosol)	espray
spray (hose)	rocío
spreader	esparcidor / bomba de asperjar
spreader (of seeds)	máquina de sembrar
sprinkler	aspersor
stake	palo
stem	tallo
steps	escaleras

stone	piedra
stoop	escalera de la entrada
storm drain	alcantarilla
string	mecate
structure	estructura
stump	tocón
sucker	chupón
sulfur	azufre
sun	sol
sunglasses	lentes de sol
sunscreen	bloqueador solar
supervisor	supervisor
supplies	productos
surface	superficie
swale	canal de desvío
swimming pool	piscina / alberca
system	sistema
tablespoon	cucharada
tarp	lona
task	tarea
taxes	impuestos
telephone	teléfono
telephone number	número de teléfono
terrace	terraza
texture	textura
things	cosas
thorns	espinas
ties	cierres
tile (floor)	baldosa
time (period)	tiempo
tips (ends)	puntas
tire	llanta
tool	herramienta
top (highest part)	la parte superior
topsoil	capa superior del suelo
town	pueblo
tow truck	grúa
tractor	tractor
trailer	remolque
trash	basura
tree	árbol
trellis	enrejado
trench	zanja / trinchera
trencher	trinche
trunk (of tree)	tronco

type	tipo
vacuum breaker	interruptor de vacío
valve	válvula
van	camioneta
vegetable	verdura
vegetation	vegetación
vine	planta trepadora
wages	sueldo
walls	paredes
water main	llave principal del agua
watering can	regadera
waterline	tubería subterránea
weed	mala hierba
weed killer	herbicida
week	semana
wheel	rueda
wheelbarrow	carretilla
wildflower	flor silvestre
window box	jardinera
wire	alambre
wood chips	pedazos de madera
worms	gusanos
wounds	heridas
wrench (adjustable)	llave inglesa
yard	jardín
year	año

Activities

Note: In this section, the words for activities are given in their "infinitive" form, the basic dictionary form, and one that does not indicate "who" is doing the action. In the text of the book, most of the "action words" are given in command form, appropriate for giving instructions.

aerate	airear
apply (a substance)	aplicar
approach	acercarse
ask	preguntar
ask for	pedir
be (a hard worker)	ser (trabajador)

English-Spanish Glossary

be (here)	estar (aquí)
be (late)	llegar (tarde)
be able	poder
blow	soplar
brake	frenar
break up (soil)	desmoronar
bring	traer
broadcast	diseminar
burn	quemar
buy	comprar
call	llamar
change	cambiar
check	checar
clean up	limpiar
close	cerrar
come	venir
come back (return)	regresar / volver
concentrate	poner atención
contact	contactar
cover	cubrir
de-thatch	airear
disinfect	desinfectar
dispose	tirar
disturb (plants)	afectar
do	hacer
drain	drenar
drink	tomar
drive	manejar
dry	secar
dry out	deshidratar
eliminate	eliminar
fasten	amarrar
fill	llenar
fill in	rellenar
finish	terminar
fire (an employee)	despedir
follow	seguir
get	obtener
get along	llevarse bien
get sick	enfermarse
give	dar
go	ir
harvest	cosechar
have	tener
help	ayudar

English-Spanish Glossary

hire	contratar
hurt oneself	lastimarse
join	juntar
keep	mantener
last (for a period of time)	durar
leave (go away)	irse
leave (something)	dejar
level	nivelar
live	vivir
lock up	cerrar con llave
look for	buscar
lubricate	lubricar
maintain	mantener
make sure	asegurarse
may / can	poder
meet (for an appointment)	encontrar
move	mover
mow	cortar el césped
need	necesitar
open	abrir
patch	parchar
pick (vegetables, fruit)	cosechar
pick up	buscar / recoger
place (put)	colocar
provide	proporcionar
put on	ponerse
raze	arrasar
remove	quitar
replace	reemplazar
return	regresar / volver
scatter	salpicar
shake	sacudir
shape	formar
sharpen	afilar
show	mostrar / enseñar
smoke	fumar
sow	sembrar
spray	asperjar
start	empezar / iniciar
start (a machine)	arrancar
stop	parar
take (to another place)	llevar
taper	afilar
tear down	desmantelar
tell	decir

thin out	aclarar / deshijar
throw	tirar
touch	tocar
treat	tratar
trim	podar
turn around	darse una vuelta
turn off (lights)	apagar
turn off (machine)	parar
turn off (water)	cerrar la llave del agua
turn on (light)	encender (la luz)
turn on (water)	abrir la llave del agua
understand	entender
use	usar
vary	variar
wait	esperar
watch	mirar / ver
wear	llevar / usar
weed	desherbar
wet	mojar
work	trabajar
wrap	envolver

Words That Tell *Whose*

her	su, sus
hers	suyo-a-os-as
his	su, sus, suyo-a-os-as
John's	de John
mine	mío-a-os-as
my	mi, mis
our, ours	nuestro-a-os-as
own (belonging to)	propio-a-os-as
theirs	suyo-a-os-as
your	su, sus
yours	suyo-a-os-as

Words That Tell *Where*

across from	enfrente de
along (the path)	a lo largo de (la sendera)
at	en
back (direction)	para atrás

behind	detrás de
between	entre
down there	abajo
downstairs	abajo
far away	lejos de aquí
far	lejos
forward	adelante
here	aquí
home (at)	en casa
home (toward)	a casa
in	en
in back of	detrás de
in front of	delante de
inside	adentro
left (direction)	a la izquierda
near	cerca
nearby	cerca de aquí
next to	al lado de
on	en
on top of	encima de
out of	fuera de
outside	afuera
over there	allí
right (direction)	a la derecha
straight ahead	todo derecho
there	ahí
through	por
to the left	a la izquierda
to the right	a la derecha
under	debajo de
underneath	debajo de
up there	arriba
upstairs	arriba

Words That Tell *How*

backward	al revés
bad / badly	mal
by hand	a mano
carefully	con cuidado
evenly	uniformemente
faster	más rápido
firmly	firmemente
gently	suavemente

lightly	ligeramente
like this / like that	así
separately	por separado
slowly	despacio / lento
so-so	más o menos
together	juntos -as
well	bien

Words That Tell *When*

advance, in	por adelantado
afterward	después
all day	todo el día
always	siempre / en todo momento
April, in	en abril
at all times	en todo momento
at six o'clock	a las seis
at the end	al final
at the same time	al mismo tiempo
August, in	en agosto
beforehand	antes
daily	todos los días
December, in	en diciembre
during the day	durante el día
early	temprano
ever	alguna vez
every day	todos los días
February, in	en febrero
first	primero
frequently	con frecuencia
Friday, on	el viernes
hour	hora
January, in	en enero
July, in	en julio
June, in	en junio
late	tarde
later	más tarde
March, in	en marzo
May, in	en mayo
midnight, at	a medianoche
Monday, on	el lunes
never	nunca
next month	el mes próximo

next week	la semana próxima
next year	el año próximo
noon, at	a mediodía
November, in	en noviembre
now	ahora
October, in	en octubre
often	con frecuencia
on Monday	el lunes
on Mondays	los lunes
on the 3rd of January	el tres de enero
on time	en punto
promptly	cuanto antes
regularly	con regularidad
right away	en seguida / ahora mismo
Saturday, on	el sábado
September, in	en septiembre
soon	pronto
Sunday, on	el domingo
Thursday, on	el jueves
today	hoy
Tuesday, on	el martes
until	hasta
Wednesday, on	el miércoles
while	mientras

Words That Tell *How Much* or *How Many*

There is / There are	Hay
a few	unos pocos, unas pocas
a little	un poco
a lot	mucho –a
extra	extra
just	sólo
less	menos
little (amount)	poco
many	muchos –as
more	más
more than (ten)	más de (diez)
one, two, etc.	uno, dos, etc.
one-half	la mitad
one-third	la tercera parte
only	solamente / sólo
several	varios -as

too many	demasiado-a-os-as
too much	demasiado -a
various	varios -as

Little Words

alone	solo -a
apart	a una distancia de
around	alrededor de
at	en
because	porque
before	antes
extra	extra
if	si
maybe	quizás
per	por
that	ese, esa
these	estas, estos
this	este, esta
those	esas, esos
to	a
with me	conmigo
with (you, him, her, etc.)	con (usted, él, ella, etc.)
without	sin

Words That Describe People, Places, or Things

Note: the endings of these words may change to match the gender or number of the words they describe.

acidic	ácido-a-os-as
alert	alerta
alkaline	alcalino-a-os-as
automatic	automático-a-os-as
bad	malo-a-os-as
beautiful	bonito-a-os-as
bigger	más grande -s
broken	roto-a-os-as
chain-link	de tela metálica
cloudy	está nublado
cold (weather)	hace frío

English-Spanish Glossary

commercial	comercial -es
cordless	inalámbrico-a-os-as
corrugated	ondulado-a-os-as
dangerous	peligroso-a-os-as
dead	muerto-a-os-as
deep	hondo-a-os-as
diagonal	diagonal -es
diseased	enfermo-a-os-as
dump	basurero / tiradero
entire	entero-a-os-as
established	establecido-a-os-as
fallen	caído-a-os-as
fine (not sick)	bien
fine (weather)	hace buen tiempo
first (most important)	primordial -es
flush	alineado-a-os-as
galvanized	galvanizado-a-os-as
good	bueno-a-os-as
granular	granular
healthy	sano-a-os-as
heavy (weight)	pesado-a-os-as
heavy (thick)	grueso-a-os-as
high	alto-a-os-as
horizontal	horizontal -es
hot (weather)	hace calor
important	importante -s
infected	infectado-a-os-as
invisible	invisible -s
large	grande -s
leather	de cuero
long	largo-a-os-as
low	bajo-a-os-as
metal	alambrado-a-os-as
multiple	múltiple -s
nearest	más cercano-a-os-as
necessary	necesario-a-os-as
new	nuevo-a-os-as
organic	orgánico-a-os-as
original	original -es
plastic	de plástico
poisonous	venenoso-a-os-as
private	particular -es
public	público-a-os-as
punctual	puntual -es
raining, it's	está lloviendo

English-Spanish Glossary

ripe	maduro-a-os-as
rounded	redondo-a-os-as
same	mismo-a-os-as
shallow	poco profundo-a-os-as
sharp (blade)	afilado-a-os-as
short	corto-a-os-as
single	sencillo-a-os-as
skilled	capicitado-a-os-as
slippery	resbaloso-a-os-as
small	pequeño-a-os-as
snowing, it's	está nevando
square	cuadrado-a-os-as
steel-toe	con punta de hierro
straight	recto-a-os-as
sunny, it's	hace sol
tall	alto-a-os-as
threaded	roscado-a-os-as
underground	subterráneo-a-os-as
unskilled	sin especialización
urgent	urgente -s
vertical	vertical -es
vital	imprescindible -s
weak	débil -es
wet	mojado-a-os-as
wide	ancho-a-os-as
windy, it's	hace viento
wooden	de madera
yellow	amarillo-a-os-as

Glosario español-inglés

Expresiones

Adiós	Good-bye
¿Adónde...?	Where to . . . ?
Bienvenido	Welcome
Buenas noches	Good evening / Good night
Buenas tardes	Good afternoon
¿Cómo...?	How . . . ?
¿Cómo está usted?	How are you?
¿Cómo se dice...?	How do you say . . . ?
¿Con quién...?	Who with . . . ?
¿Cuál...?	What . . . ? (name, telephone number)
¿Cuándo...?	When . . . ?
¿Cuánto...?	How much . . . ?
¿Cuántos...?	How many . . . ?
Cuidado. / Tenga cuidado.	Be careful.
¿De dónde...?	Where from . . . ?
de la mañana	A.M.
de la noche	P.M.
de la tarde	P.M.
de nada	You're welcome
¿De quién...?	Whose . . . ?
Disculpe.	Excuse me.
¿Dónde...?	Where . . . ?
en caso de una emergencia	in case of an emergency
Gracias.	Thank you.
¿Hasta cuándo...?	Until when . . . ?
Hasta luego.	See you later.
Hola.	Hello.
Llame al nueve-uno-uno.	Call 9-1-1.
Lo siento.	I'm sorry.
No...	Don't . . .
No	No
¡Ojalá!	God willing
¿Para qué...?	What for . . . ?
¿Por cuánto tiempo...?	For how long . . . ?
Por favor	Please
¿Por qué?	Why?

¿Qué...?	What . . . ? (thing)
¿Qué hora es?	What time is it?
¿Quién...?	Who . . . ?
Sí	Yes

Personas

albañil	bricklayer
alguien	someone
amigo, amiga	friend
él	he
ella	she
ellos / ellas	they
esposa	wife
esposo	husband
expertos en irrigación	irrigation experts
familia	family
hermana	sister
hermano	brother
hija	daughter
hijo	son
hijos, hijas	children (sons and daughters)
instalador de tuberías	pipe layer
jardinero, jardinera	gardener
jefe	boss
la	her
le	to her / him / you
lo	him
mamá / madre	mother
nadie	nobody
niño, niña	child
niños, niñas	children
nosotros / nosotras	we
novia	girlfriend
novio	boyfriend
obrero	laborer
padres	parents
papá / padre	father
patrón	boss
trabajador /trabajadora	worker
usted	you
ustedes	you all
vecino, vecina	neighbor
yo	I

Lugares

acera	sidewalk
afueras de la ciudad	suburbs
almacén de la madera	lumberyard
apartamento	apartment
área	area
autopista	highway
banqueta	curb
baño	bathroom, restroom
basurero	dump
calle	street
camino	road
campo	countryside
cancha de golf	golf course
cantera	quarry
carretera	highway, road
casa	house
centro comercial	shopping center
ciudad	city
club privado	country club
condominio	condominium
departamento	apartment
edificio	building
edificio público	office building
entrada	driveway / entrance
escuela	school
esquina	corner (outside)
estación de trenes	train station
ferretería	hardware store
fondo	bottom
hospital	hospital
jardín	garden
oficina	office
parada de autobuses	bus stop
parcela	lot
parque	park
parque de recreo para niños	playground
patio	patio
rincón	corner (inside)
sendero	path
sitio de trabajo	jobsite
tiradero	dump
townhouse	town house
vereda	path
vivero	nursery

Cosas

abrigo	coat
accidente	accident
aceite	oil
actitud	attitude
adaptador	adapter
alambre	wire
alberca	swimming pool
alcantarilla	sewer / storm drain
alcohol	alcohol
almuerzo	lunch
alto-a-os-as	high
altura	height
aluminio	aluminum foil
ambulancia	ambulance
animal	animal
antisifón	antisiphon
año	year
arado	plow
árbol	tree
arbusto	bush
arena	sand
arriate	flower bed
aspersor	sprinkler
aspersor del aceite de dormancia	dormant oil spray
aumento	raise
ayuda	help / assistance
azadón	hoe
azufre	sulfur
babosa	slug
baldosa	tile (floor)
baleros	bearings
barro	clay pottery
basura	trash
basurero	dump
batería	battery (car, truck)
biper	beeper
bisagra	hinge
bloque hueco de cemento	concrete block
bloqueador solar	sunscreen
bola	ball
bolsa	bag
bomba de asperjar	spreader
boquilla de salida	nozzle

Glosario español-inglés

borde	border / edging
botas	boots
brotes	shoots
bujías	spark plugs
bulbo	bulb
cable	cable
cables para pasar corriente	jumper cables
café	coffee
caída	fall
cal	lime
camión de volteo	dump truck
camioneta	pickup truck / van
canal de desvío	diversion gutter / swale
canaleta	gutter
capa superior del suelo	topsoil
capullo	cocoon / flower bud
caracol	snail
carretilla	wheelbarrow
casco	hard hat
cebos	baits
cemento	cement / mortar
cepas de pasto	plugs (of grass)
cerámica	pottery
cerca	fence
cerco	fence
cerco verde	hedge
césped	sod
cheque	check
chupón	sucker
cierres	ties
cinturón	belt
cipellón	root ball
círculo	circle
clavo	nail
cliente	client
collar	collar
combustible diesel	diesel fuel
compañía	company
compuerta	retaining wall
compuesto de juntas	joint compound
comunidad	community
concreto	concrete
conector de codo	elbow connection
conglomerados	aggregate
contenedor para escombros	dumpster

Glosario español-inglés

control	control
cortabordes	edger
cortada	clippings
cortadora con asiento	riding lawnmower
cortadora de césped	lawnmower
cortadora de motor	power lawn mower
cortadora de ruedas altas	high-wheel lawn mower
cortadora manual	push lawn mower
corteza de pino	pine bark
cosas	things
costuras	seams
cucharada	tablespoon
cultivadora rotatoria	rotary tiller
dedo	finger
descanso	break (rest period)
desmenusador	mulcher
dinero	money
diseño	design
documentos	documents
dólares	dollars
drenaje	drain
drenaje de barro	drain tile
drogas	drugs
durmientes de ferrocarril	railroad ties
efectivo	cash
eje	axle
embriague	clutch
emergencia	emergency
enrejado	trellis
entrada	stoop / entrance
equipo	equipment
escaleras	steps
escombro	debris
esparcidor	spreader
espinas	thorns
espray	spray (aerosol)
estaca	stake
estanque	man-made pond
estiércol	manure
estructura	structure
excavadora	backhoe
felpa	felt (cloth)
fertilizante	fertilizer
fieltro	felt
fila	row

Glosario español-inglés

filtradora de aire	respirator
filtro	filter
flor	flower
flor silvestre	wildflower
fósforo	phosphorus
fuga de combustible	fuel leak
fungicida	fungicide
galón	gallon
gasolina	gasoline
gato (para levantar el carro)	jack
gobierno	government
grava	gravel
grifo de manguera	sill cock
grúa	tow truck
guantes	gloves
gusanos	worms
habilidades	skills
hacha	axe
herbicida	weed killer
heridas	wounds
herramienta	tool
hiedra	ivy
hierba	herb
hoja	leaf / blade
hoyo	hole
hueco	hole
impuestos	taxes
insecticida	insecticide
instrucciones	instructions
interruptor de vacío	vacuum breaker
irrigación	irrigation
jardín	garden / yard
jardinera	planter / window box
la parte superior	top (highest part)
ladrillo	brick
laguna	natural pond
lecciones	lessons
lentes de seguridad	goggles
lentes de sol	sunglasses
levantamiento de objetos pesados	heavy lifting
licencia de manejar	driver's license
línea	row
línea de agua	waterline
líquido	liquid
llanta	tire

Glosario español-inglés

llave inglesa	wrench (adjustable)
llave principal del agua	water main
lona	tarp
loza	flagstone
lugar	place
maceta	flowerpot
mala hierba	weed
maleza	brush
malla	netting
manguera chorreando	hose (drip)
manguera de remojo	hose (soaker)
máquina	machine
máquina de sembrar	spreader (of seeds)
máscara	face shield / mask
materia	matter / substance
mecate	binding / string
mes	month
minuto	minute
moho	mold
mordaza de tipo tornillo	clamp (screw-type)
mordaza para mangueras	clamp (hose)
mordaza para tuberías	clamp (pipe)
motor	engine / motor
natural	natural
negocio	business
nido de pájaros	bird's nest
nieve	snow
nitrógeno	nitrogen
nombre	name
pala	spade / shovel
pala de mano	hand spade
pala para la nieve	snow shovel
pantalones	pants
papel	paper
paredes	walls
parte	part
pasador	latch
pedazo	piece
pedazos de hielo	icicles
pedazos de madera	wood chips
peligro	danger
pentanol	penta / pentanol
piedra	stone /rock
piedras	pebbles
piel	skin

piezas	slabs
pigmento	pigment
pila	battery (small) /pile
pila de composta	compost pile
pintar	paint
piscina	swimming pool
pizarra	slate
planta anual	annual
planta perenne	perennial
planta que da flores	flowering plant
planta trepadora	vine
plantas de cobertura	ground cover
plantita	seedling
podado, lo	clippings
podadoras	clippers
polvo	powder / dust
poste de madera	wooden post
potasio	potassium
primeros auxilios	first aid
privacidad	privacy
problema	problem
producto	product / supply
producto de juntas	joint compound
profundidad	depth
protección	protection
protector de oídos	earmuffs
proyecto	project
pueblo	town
puerta	gate / door
pulgada	inch
puntas	tips (ends)
productos químicos	chemicals
raíz	root
rama	branch
rastrillo	rake
reciclaje	recycling
recipiente	container
recogedor de cortada	grass-catcher
referencia	reference
refresco	soft drink
regadera	watering can
remolque	trailer
repelente para insectos	insect repellant
respiradora	respirator
riegos	irrigation

Glosario español-inglés

rocío	spray (hose)
rueda	wheel
sal	salt
seguridad	safety
semana	week
semillas	seeds
señales	signals
seto vivo	hedge
sierra	saw
sistema	system
sol	sun
sombra	shade
sombrero	sun hat
sopladora de hojas	leaf blower
sopladora para la nieve	snowblower
sueldo	wages / pay / salary
superficie	surface
supervisor	supervisor
surco	furrow
sustrato	mulch / leaf mold / peat moss
tallo	stem
tapones para los oídos	earplugs
tarea	chore / errand / assignment / task
techo	roof
teléfono	telephone / telephone number
terraza	terrace
terrenos	grounds
terrón	clump
textura	texture
tiempo	time (period) / weather
tierra	earth / ground / soil
tijeras de mango largo	loppers
tijeras de podar	pruners
tipo	type
tiradero	dump
tocón	stump
tormenta	storm
trabajo	job
tractor	tractor
tractor para el césped	lawn tractor
trapo	cloth / rag
trinche	trencher / fork (garden)
tronco	tree trunk
tuberías	pipes
tubos de drenaje	drain pipes

válvula	valve
válvula de drenaje	drain valve
vegetación	vegetation
verdura	vegetable
vivero	nursery
yeso	plaster
zanja	ditch / trench
zapatos	shoes

Actividades

Note: In this section, the words for activities are given in their "infinitive" form, the basic dictionary form, and one that does not indicate "who" is doing the action. In the text of the book, most of the "action words" are given in command form, appropriate for giving instructions.

abrir	open
abrir la llave del agua	turn on the water
acercarse	approach
aclarar	thin out
afilar	sharpen / taper
airear	aerate / de-thatch
amarrar	fasten
apagar	turn off (lights)
aplicar	apply (a substance)
arrancar	start (a machine)
arrasar	raze
asegurarse	make sure
asperjar	spray
ayudar	help
buscar	look for / go get
cambiar	change
cerrar	close
cerrar con llave	lock up
cerrar la llave del agua	turn off the water
checar	check
colocar	place / put
comprar	buy
contactar	contact
contratar	hire

Glosario español-inglés

cortar el césped	mow
cosechar	pick (vegetables) / harvest
cubrir	cover
dar	give
darse una vuelta	turn around
decir	tell
dejar	leave (something)
desherbar	weed
deshidrator	dry out
deshijar	thin out
desinfectar	disinfect
desmantelar	tear down
desmoronar	break up
despedir	fire
diseminar	broadcast
drenar	drain
durar	last (for a period of time)
eliminar	eliminate
empezar	start
encender	turn on (lights)
enfermarse	get sick
enseñar	show / teach
entender	understand
envolver	wrap
esperar	wait
estar (aquí)	be (here)
afectar	disturb
formar	shape
frenar	brake
fumar	smoke
hacer	do
hacer un desnivel	slope
iniciar	start
ir	go
irse	leave (go away)
juntar	join
lastimarse	hurt oneself
limpiar	clean / clean up
llamar	call
llegar (tarde)	be (late)
llenar	fill
llevar	wear / carry / take
llevarse bien	get along
lubricar	lubricate
manejar	drive

Glosario español-inglés

mantener	keep / maintain
mirar	watch / look at
mojar	wet
mostrar	show
mover	move
nivelar	level
amarrar	fasten
obtener	get
parar	stop / turn off (machine)
parchar	patch
pedir	ask for
podar	trim / prune
poder	be able / may / can
ponerse	wear / put on
poner atención	concentrate
preguntar	ask
proporcionar	provide
quemar	burn
quitar	remove
recoger	pick up
reemplazar	replace
regresar	come back (return)
rellenar	fill in
sacudir	shake
salpicar	spray / scatter
secar	dry
seguir	follow
sembrar	plant seeds
ser (trabajador)	be (a hard worker)
soplar	blow
tener	have
terminar	finish
tirar	throw / dispose of
tocar	touch
tomar	drink
trabajar	work
traer	bring
tratar	treat
usar	use
variar	vary
venir	come
ver	come back (return)

Palabras que indican *de quién*

mi, mis	my
mío-a-os-as	mine
nuestro-a-os-as	our, ours
propio-a-os-as	own (belonging to)
su, sus	her / his / your / their
suyo-a-os-as	hers / his / yours / theirs

Palabras que indican *dónde*

a casa	toward home
a la derecha	to the right
a la izquierda	to the left
a lo largo de (la vereda)	along (the path)
abajo	down there / downstairs
adelante	forward
adentro	inside
afuera	outside
ahí	there
al lado de	next to
allí	over there
aquí	here
arriba	up there / upstairs
cerca	near
cerca de aquí	nearby
debajo de	under / underneath
delante de	in front of
detrás de	in back of / behind
en	in / on / at
en casa	at home
encima de	on top of
enfrente de	across from
entre	between
fuera de	out of
lejos (de aquí)	far / far away
para atrás	back (direction)
por	through
todo derecho	straight ahead

Palabras que indican *cómo*

a mano	by hand
al revés	backward
así	like this / like that
bien	well
con cuidado	carefully
despacio	slowly
firmemente	firmly
juntos -as	together
lento	slowly
ligeramente	lightly
mal	bad, badly
más o menos	so-so
más rápido	faster
por separado	separately
suavemente	gently
uniformemente	evenly

Palabras que indican *cuándo*

a las seis	at six o'clock
abril, en	in April
agosto, en	in August
ahora	now
ahora mismo	right away
al final	at the end
al mismo tiempo	at the same time
alguna vez	ever
antes	beforehand
con frecuencia	frequently / often
con regularidad	regularly
cuanto antes	promptly
después	afterward
diciembre, en	in December
domingo, el	on Sunday
durante el día	during the day
el año próximo	next year
el lunes	on Monday
el mes próximo	next month
el tres de enero	on the 3rd of January
en punto	on time
en seguida	right away
en todo momento	at all times

enero, en	in January
febrero, en	in February
hasta _____	until _____
hora	hour / time
hoy	today
jueves, el	on Thursday
julio, en	in July
junio, en	in June
la semana próxima	next week
los lunes	on Mondays
lunes, el	on Monday
martes, el	on Tuesday
marzo, en	in March
más tarde	later
mayo, en	in May
medianoche, a	at midnight
mediodía, a	at noon
mientras _____	while _____
miércoles, el	on Wednesday
noviembre, en	in November
nunca	never
octubre, en	in October
por adelantado	in advance
primero	first
pronto	soon
sábado, el	on Saturday
septiembre, en	in September
siempre	always
tarde	late
temprano	early
todo el día	all day
todos los días	daily / every day
viernes, el	on Friday

Palabras que indican *cuánto* o *cuántos*

demasiado-a-os-as	too many
demasiado -a	too much
extra	extra
Hay	There is / There are
la mitad	one-half
la tercera parte	one-third
más	more
más de (diez)	more than (ten)

menos	less
mucho -a	a lot
muchos -as	many
poco	little (amount)
pocos -as	few
un poco	a little
uno, dos, etc.	one, two, etc.
unos pocos, unas pocas	a few
varios-a-os-as	several / various

Palabras pequeñas

a	to
a una distancia de	apart
alrededor	around
antes	before
con (usted, él, ella, etc.)	with (you, him, her, etc.)
conmigo	with me
en	in / on / at
esas, esos	those
ese, esa	that
estas, estos	these
este, esta	this
extra	extra
por	per / through
porque	because
quizás	maybe
si	if
sin	without
solo -a	alone
sólo	only, just
solamente	only, just

Palabras que describen las personas, los lugares, o las cosas

ácido-a-os-as	acidic
afilado-a-os-as	sharp (blade)
alambrado-a-os-as	of metal / wire
alcalino-a-os-as	alkaline
alerta -s	alert
alineado-a-os-as	flush
alto-a-os-as	tall /high

Glosario español-inglés

amarillo-a-os-as	yellow
ancho-a-os-as	wide
automático-a-os-as	automatic
bajo-a-os-as	low
bien	fine (not sick)
bonito-a-os-as	beautiful
buen tiempo, hace	it's fine (weather)
bueno-a-os-as	good
caído-a-os-as	fallen
calor, hace	it's hot (weather)
capicitado-a-os-as	skilled
comercial -es	commercial
con punta de hierro	steel-toe
corrugado-a-os-as	corrugated
corto-a-os-as	short
cuadrado-a-os-as	square
de cuero	of leather
de madera	wooden
de plástico	plastic
de tela metálica	chain-link
débil -es	weak
desmenusador -a	mulcher
diagonal -es	diagonal
enfermo-a-os-as	diseased, sick
entero-a-os-as	entire
establecido-a-os-as	established
frío, hace	it's cold
galvanizado-a-os-as	galvanized
grande -s	large
granular	granular
grueso-a-os-as	heavy (thick)
hondo-a-os-as	deep
horizontal -es	horizontal
importante -s	important
imprescindible -s	vital
inalámbrico-a-os-as	cordless
infectado-a-os-as	infected
invisible -s	invisible
largo-a-os-as	long
lloviendo, está	it's raining
maduro-a-os-as	ripe
malo-a-os-as	bad
más cercano-a-os-as	nearest
más grande -s	bigger
mismo-a-os-as	same

Glosario español-inglés

mojado-a-os-as	wet
muerto-a-os-as	dead
multiple -s	multiple
necesario-a-os-as	necessary
nevando, está	it's snowing
no especializado-a-os-as	unskilled
nublado, está	it's cloudy
nuevo-a-os-as	new
orgánico-a-os-as	organic
original -es	original
particular -es	private
peligroso-a-os-as	dangerous
pequeño-a-os-as	small
pesado-a-os-as	heavy
poco profundo-a-os-as	shallow
primordial	most important
público-a-os-as	public
puntual -es	punctual
recto-a-os-as	straight
redondo-a-os-as	rounded
resbaloso-a-os-as	slippery
roscado-a-os-as	threaded
roto-a-os-as	broken
sano-a-os-as	healthy
sencillo-a-os-as	single / simple
sin especialización	unskilled
sol, hace	it's sunny
subterráneo-a-os-as	underground
urgente -s	urgent
venenoso-a-os-as	poisonous
vertical -es	vertical
viento, hace	it's windy
voleo, al	randomly